SUDDENLY SINGLE AFTER 50

SUDDENLY SINGLE AFTER 50

The Girlfriends' Guide to Navigating Loss, Restoring Hope, and Rebuilding Your Life

Barbara Ballinger and Margaret Crane

ROWMAN & LITTLEFIELD
Lanham • Boulder • New York • London

Published by Rowman & Littlefield
A wholly owned subsidiary of The Rowman & Littlefield Publishing Group, Inc.
4501 Forbes Boulevard, Suite 200, Lanham, Maryland 20706
www.rowman.com

Unit A, Whitacre Mews, 26-34 Stannary Street, London SE11 4AB

British Library Cataloguing in Publication Information Available

Library of Congress Cataloging-in-Publication Data

Names: Ballinger, Barbara (Barbara B.) author. | Crane, Margaret, author.
Title: Suddenly single after 50 : the girlfriends' guide to navigating loss, restoring hope, and
     rebuilding your life / Barbara Ballinger and Margaret Crane.
Other titles: Suddenly single after fifty
Description: Lanham : Rowman & Littlefield, 2016. | Includes bibliographical references.
Identifiers: LCCN 2015045829 (print) | LCCN 2015047600 (ebook) | ISBN 9781442256521
     (cloth : alk. paper) | ISBN 9781442256538 (electronic)
Subjects: LCSH: Single women. | Single women--Life skills guides. | Self-actualization (Psycholo-
     gy)
Classification: LCC HQ800.2 .B355 2016 (print) | LCC HQ800.2 (ebook) | DDC 306.81/53--dc23
LC record available at http://lccn.loc.gov/2015045829

Printed in the United States of America

For my daughters. Joanna and Lucy, my mother, Estelle, and my many female friends who surrounded me with friendship and love.

To my children, Adam, Remy and Tommy, and the memory of their father, Nolan Crane. I miss him every day.

CONTENTS

ACKNOWLEDGMENTS

This is our story and everywoman's story of losing a spouse or life partner. We're two good friends and writing partners for more than 30 years who had parallel heartbreaking experiences. We both lost our spouses, one to divorce and the other to death. After we grieved—cried, shut down, raged, and picked ourselves up, moving from almost inconsolable sadness to healthfulness and happiness again—we resolved to share our stories and what we each learned with others who are fifty-plus and navigating a new life after a spousal or partner loss.

There are many people we wish to thank. Friends and family encouraged us to write this book. "There is such a need for this," was the typical response when we talked about our idea. When we started this project three years ago after saving hundreds of e-mails between us, spending hours coming up with ideas, titles, anecdotes, an outline, a first and then a second draft of our manuscript, friends and family enthusiastically offered to read portions or let us read chapters out loud to them.

Many ideas to fine tune chapters or add this and that came from various sources, and we would be remiss not to mention certain friends and family: Susan eagerly read multiple early versions and made countless suggestions verbally and in writing; Marilyn read many early chapters and later listened to more refined versions and gave us the green light; another friend and lawyer Lisa also approved content, including legalese; Barbara's younger daughter Lucy read the entire manuscript and gave us the nod; Margaret's sister, Mary Anne, a tough and wise critic, offered her counsel and expertise and, most importantly, her approval; Debbie read two chapters and offered some edits and suggestions; business colleague Irina encouraged us from the get-go after reading some early chapters; and June read some chapters and the proposal and was very encouraging and helpful with her suggestions.

Special thanks also goes to our former literary agent Danielle Egan-Miller who read our proposal and said it's good but not for me. Thank you for directing us to our wonderful literary agent Kelli Christenson. She offered both editing and/or literary agent help, and we said, "We'll take both!" Kelli revised our proposal, made it shine, added some humor, and found us a publisher within a month of submitting the proposal and after only seven rejections, fewer she informed us than J. K. Rowling who received twelve before she found a home for *Harry Potter*. We only should see such success!

Also, thanks to the ever-present and often unheralded public libraries, where we did research. One of us even learned how to tweet cost free, with a very kind and patient trainer, Andrew Bono. Thanks as well to Alison Green who set up our weekly Weblog, www.lifelessonsat50plus.com, and gave us a tutorial in how to handle the mechanics of it.

Thanks as well to our publisher's editor Suzanne Staszak-Silva and Laura Reiter, production editor. We couldn't have done it without your comments, suggestions, patience, and compliments to keep us going.

We want to thank those who fact-checked our information: Dr. Armin Ghobadi, assistant professor, medicine, Division of Oncology and Section of Bone Marrow Transplant at the Washington University's School of Medicine; Mueriel Carp, director of community relations and events, Siteman Cancer Center; Jim Goodwin, associate director of cancer news, Siteman Cancer Center; Sherry Delo and Judy Rubin, principals/partners at Plaza Advisory Group; and Cary Mogerman with the law firm Zerman Mogerman LLC.

Thanks to the therapists who helped us find our way: to Peggy, Denton, Mike, and Jan, and grief support group counselor, Mary.

To the many women who we talked to who have also lost their spouses or life partners to death or divorce and told us their stories, we thank you for your time and honesty. And finally, to all women who have lost a spouse or life partner and whose stories go untold, we hope you'll continue to tell them in your own way on your own timetable while going through the healing processes and that you'll use this book as a tool. Each of us has our own way of coping and moving on, but we can say unequivocally, there is life after loss.

As always, we're grateful for the love, encouragement, and tolerance of all our family members—parents, kids, siblings, and cousins—who embraced this idea and our words, which brought back living through great sadness for all of us. Yet, they understood writing this book and our weekly blog have been part of our healing, and we hope will heal so many others. These are our writing legacies and true-life lessons.

Through it all, our new partners stood by our sides. You've listened and read, too—believed in us, cheered us on, offered critiques about the legal and financial parts of the book, and some of the emotional content—continue to love us, and make us laugh when humor is sorely needed to add levity. Quite simply, you've been instrumental in helping us find our way after being lost.

Barbara Ballinger and Margaret Crane, 2016

FOREWORD

In this touching memoir/instruction manual, Barbara and Margaret give an honest look at what it means to navigate life after 50. Holding almost nothing back, the two share their deeply personal stories of suffering, denial, and loss—all of us can relate. They touch on the pain, but do not dwell on it. They instead offer strategies to rise and move forward without preaching or judging.

No topic is too sacred to remain unexplored. And in a world, in which social taboos often preclude open discussions about sex, death, money, and taxes, it is refreshing to read *Suddenly Single After 50*; nothing is off limits. For example, I understood the absence of a magic formula or preset timetable for handling loss (having had my own personal experiences), but I never explicitly told people what to say and how to say it. It is hard to offer that kind of advice! But Barbara and Margaret have mastered the art. With humorous yet precise bullet lists like:

What to say and what not to say to a friend whose spouse is ill?
How to write an online dating profile?
How to eat alone?
And, of course, when do you fix the faucet or hire a handyman?
I learned so much and so will you.

These two women are just like you and me. By midlife, we all know from personal experience that life is complicated, messy, and often painful. However, we often forget that we have choices. We can dwell on why this happened or we can figure out what do to next. In *Suddenly Single After 50*, Barbara and Margaret undoubtedly empower each of us to choose the latter.

By the way, in case you read the last pages first (as I often do), spoiler alert: There is no fairy-tale ending. That would be far too clichéd for these sophisticated authors. Rather, there is hope. And what we all really want at the end of the day is just that, the belief that tomorrow will be better because we took action today. With *Suddenly Single After 50*, you will have the tools to make your lives better!

May you find love.

May you find hope.

And if you are lost, may you be found.

Sherre Hirsch
Rabbi and Author of *Thresholds: How to Thrive through Life's Transitions to Live Fearlessly and Regret-Free* and
We Plan, God Laughs: What to Do When Life Hits You Over the Head.
Los Angeles, California

INTRODUCTION

Two Friends: A Parallel Journey

Barbara's marriage didn't end overnight. It happened slowly as her husband stepped further and further away from their shared life. No grocery store shopping together, no attending recitals and confirmations for their two daughters as a duo, and more days away for his work. "You must have known what was happening?" everyone later asked. But she didn't see what was right under her nose. She was too busy writing, being a mother to their two teenage daughters, and, she thought, the original good wife, who married right out of college at age twenty-two. And then, poof. After three major moves and twenty-nine years of marriage, she was unceremoniously dumped on a warm Saturday afternoon when her then-husband turned to her in their remodeled kitchen and announced: "The passion is gone."

Margaret lost her spouse and love of her life after a five-year-illness that ended their forty-two years together. One illness, then another, and finally a third, with Nolan fighting fiercer as his days dwindled. He kept insisting his medical team try some new course of chemotherapy or find a clinical trial. Margaret fought alongside him. Even a week before he died, she believed a cure would be found, and they would live together happily and share in the joys and vicissitudes of their three adult children's lives for many decades to come.

Along with our collective losses came a rush of emotions—tears, anger, self-pity. Why us? We got up each morning, looked in the mirror and realized that suddenly we had twenty-something, saddened hearts lodged in fifty-plus aging, sagging bodies. To put on a happy face to go out into the world and face family, friends, and colleagues didn't seem feasible. Looming in our new lives were all sorts of frightening possibilities. We wondered:

- Would we be forced to support ourselves by standing on our feet all day long as Walmart greeters, working on holidays and Saturdays to earn double overtime?
- Would we end up perusing the aisles of grocery stores on weekends reduced to looking at men's hands to see if they were wearing wedding bands, or checking their grocery carts to note whether they were buying single-serving portions—and might be our catch of the day?
- Would we be sitting at home, alone each night? After all, who would want us to contaminate their fun? Our sadness might be contagious.
- Would we each become the cliché of the single woman who becomes attracted to her contractor, painter, or plumber, in part because they were the only men in our lives and homes?
- Would we gain weight while eating so much junk food out of frustration as we watched movies alone, and then become so overweight with bad knees and aching backs that we'd never attract a member of the opposite sex—although in our enormous state we'd be hard to miss in a crowd?
- Would we ever date again (or even want to)—something so foreign to both of us after long-term marriages? What seemed most unimaginable—would we fall in love again?

And would we, feeling desperate, go against our prior thoughts and visit plastic surgeons or cosmetic dermatologists to erase wrinkles, tighten turkey necks and flabby tummies, and eradicate varicose veins?

Of course, we wondered—and worried for the long term—mostly about feeling lonely as we walked into darkened houses without anyone to greet us and missed having anyone to hug us if we woke in the middle of the night.

We were on our own. Regardless of a divorce and death, we were having parallel experiences: Our children were grown and lived out of town, our surviving parents were aging and required more help, and we'd each have to wade through decades of possessions by ourselves to decide what to keep, sell, discard, or donate as we each got our too-large, costly homes ready to sell to provide needed funds.

We also worried how we'd cope day to day. We were each married to guys who were fairly competent around the house. They took over. We never tackled a backed-up sewer, clogged dishwasher, or frozen pipe, or bought a car on our own, and knew nothing about how to play it confident so a salesman or contractor wouldn't try to pull a fast one on a vulnerable woman. That was despite the fact we'd written dozens of articles and some books about these topics. It was different when it was our home, car, and finances.

We also feared going to medical procedures on our own—prepping for a colonoscopy when there was nobody to laugh and commiserate with us as we stayed up late into the night on the toilet, and then had to decide the next day whose name to write on the dotted line for next of kin in case the surgeon punctured our colon.

We charted our new way forward, mostly out of necessity. We bravely learned to shut the door tight and stuff a towel into the opening when one of us was convinced a mouse was scampering through the hall at 11 p.m. and the exterminator refused to make a house call to help a hysterical woman.

Perhaps, one of the hardest parts has been something as simple as going to a social event alone and everyone trying to be polite and tiptoe around our sadness. The conversation goes like this:

"How are you?" someone asks caringly.

"Great! How are you?" you reply, wanting instead to cry and get away, but you don't. You know you have to deliver an Academy Award–winning performance for those who aren't in your tightest circle.

But before you can escape, like a telephoto lens, they zoom in with a soulful look and follow-up question. "Are you really OK?" clasping your hands in theirs and asking with gasping, facetious sadness.

And then all you want to do is scream: "YES, I said yes, and even if I weren't, do you think I'd tell YOU?" Of course, you don't because so few want to know the truth. They want you to be JUST FINE.

We are. But it took time, lots of time. Years. At first, the aloneness was interspersed with comic relief. We were ecstatic when the phone rang and we heard a man's voice, even if it was the driveway sealer. So what if a Saturday night meant sitting on the floor at Barnes & Noble, skim latte in hand, reading every book in the self-help section on separation, stay or go, divorce, widowhood, dating past fifty, and how to have passionate sex in a dozen positions. Look how much we learned.

We had never lived alone; one of us was in our fifties; the other past sixty when our ordeals began. There's no rule book on how to do this, so we had to create our own with the one thing neither divorce nor death could steal from us permanently—our humor. In fact, we couldn't start writing this until both of us were ready to laugh again. Because the road forward has been tough—often with several steps back and more tears than we thought possible—we wanted to share what we've learned with others. The range of challenges is extensive, from what you're entitled to from Social Security as a divorcee or widow, to the uneasiness of staying in your house at night alone the first few times, and how to start dating, get undressed in front of a man in the dark, and then dressed in the light, and have—yes, *that*, too, especially because the highest rate of STDs is occurring in our older age group.

We each lost so much, but found much more than we ever imagined. We also helped each other. Margaret and her husband Nolan were there for Barbara, encouraging her to date; listening to her many stories about the 350 guys she met, but who's counting; including her socially when they could; and keeping up her spirits with laughter and wine. And Barbara returned the favor and guided Margaret when she felt low, needed to laugh, and was ready to date despite her early insistence, "I'll never go out or do what you've done." The translation: "I'm not going to turn into a cyberslut like you," even if the American Association of Retired Persons (AARP) reports that 45 percent of adults aged sixty-five and older are divorced, separated, or widowed with this group representing the fastest-growing segment in online dating (Ellin 2014).

Now, it's our time to help you move forward, whether you have lost a spouse or life partner through death or divorce. Consider our strategy. We redefined *alone*. *Alone* means we now live by our rules. We look at all the options, possible scenarios, and a world of fresh ideas, experiences and friends, and embrace what we choose to do. We've learned most of all that our new lives are far from perfect, but we've fashioned ones that are better than eating and drinking alone and don't cause weight gain, wrinkles, clogged arteries, and 24/7 sadness. Other women's stories are also included, and many of their names and their partners' names have been changed to protect their privacy. The names of men dated reflect pseudonyms to offer them anonymity as well. In addition, we have recalled as closely as possible conversations when we didn't have detailed written records or transcribed conversations.

REFERENCE

Ellin, Abby. 2014. "Matchmakers Help Those Over 60 Handle Dating's Risks and Rewards." *New York Times*, March 28.

I

LOVE STRUCK

MARGARET

MY STORY

Outside a Baskin-Robbins ice cream shop on a warm June evening in 1966, I saw a handsome guy with a great tan dressed in white tennis attire leaning against a black MG sports car talking to a woman—obviously his date. Dawdling over their ice cream cones, her attention was casually focused on him. His gaze was on me. I was dressed in cut-off jeans and a loose T-shirt, the style at the time. I had shiny, dark brown hair parted in the middle, like Cher's, down to my waist, and my slim legs were tan from spending hours swimming and sunbathing at my girlfriend's pool.

I ignored his stare and entered the shop, engrossed in deciding what to order. After doing so, I turned to leave. And there he was. I remember thinking he was tall and very bold for coming over to me. I was guarded and not terribly friendly.

He asked for my name and phone number and left. And that was that, or so I thought. Two hours later, my phone rang. I picked it up, and Nolan Crane was on the phone. He asked me out for the next night. I couldn't go. He asked me for Friday night. I was busy. "What about the following Wednesday? This is the last time I'll ask," he warned, sounding surprised and a bit annoyed.

I accepted.

We went on our first date July 2, 1966, to hear jazz at a local pub after Nolan slipped me a fake I.D. Then we went for burgers at a drive-in diner—and that's when my life changed. We were together almost every day that July and August—listening to good music, swimming, biking, taking long walks, eating out, and sipping cheap Chianti—until I returned to college in early September for my junior year, and he returned to graduate school. During that time, I told him everything about me. He did the same. He was tall, dark, and movie-star handsome. I was hooked on his luminous, large hazel eyes with long, dark lashes, his very white teeth, dazzling smile, and sexy tush. He exuded charm and made me laugh with endless stories about his childhood, musical experiences, parents, friends, and college escapades. He was industrious and entrepreneurial and had never been handed anything, supporting himself with three jobs throughout undergraduate and graduate school—shoe salesman, working in his father's pharmacy, and playing drums in various jazz bands. As a bonus, he was a nice Jewish boy, even with a name like Nolan Crane.

Back at our separate universities, we kept in touch writing and calling. Several months later, when I came home for Christmas vacation, he met me at my front door. It was then that I fell in love for the first time.

I thought about him constantly. I brooded when he wasn't there. I waited for the phone to ring so I could hear his voice. And when we were together, I was radiant, whether we simply listened to music in his basement or at a club, where he often performed with his jazz quartet, or just taking a walk; bike riding; playing Scrabble, cards or other games; barbecuing at his house; or hitting tennis or golf balls. We'd go to rock concerts and to hear classical music and opera, see movies, go boating on the lagoon in a nearby park, picnic, and attend plays and lectures at local universities.

Falling in love like that strikes like a thunderbolt. I felt a kind of electricity when he was around that I had never experienced before. It wasn't so much passion or sex, as a desire to be with him no matter what. It just felt right. When we were together, he gave me his full attention. He knew when I was fading or tired. He knew how to make me laugh, what foods I liked. He learned to have a cup of coffee or hot chocolate waiting for me at the beginning of the day or a box of our city's best Bissinger's Chocolates at day's end. He even played my favorite operas and symphonies, not his music of choice.

A jazz aficionado, he considered classical music a cultivated white noise. Soon, music of all genres became a huge part of our lives. He'd love to hear jazz, play it over and over. He would often sit on the sofa and listen to Freddie Hubbard, Stan Kenton, Ramsey Lewis, or Wynton Marsalis, or hum a Sergio Mendes tune, drumming his fingers to the beat. He would rattle off song titles, musicians, and composers with the ease of a disc jockey. He was a musical autodidact who started collecting records from the time he was five years old. By age 12, he had become an accomplished drummer, and at 13 he started a Glenn Miller-style big band of mostly junior high and high school musicians. They were a novelty at first. Young. An ethnic mix. Soon they became quite good and were booked almost every weekend for country clubs, Bar and Bat Mitzvahs, weddings, and private parties.

I loved that about him. I loved learning about him. I loved learning new things with him. He opened up new worlds for me as I did for him, too—whether music, politics or something as prosaic as how to plant tulip bulbs or make chewy rather than crispy chocolate chip cookies.

In short order, we went from being strangers to familiar pals, into a close loving relationship, and then to commitment, marriage, domesticity, and respect. Being in love with Nolan was accompanied by a sense of rightness I had never felt before, and we decided to marry after dating for two and a half years. I was only 22 years old; he was 26.

Our wedding was huge, much to my chagrin, but Nolan had a large family and wanted to include everyone he could. So, I went along as my mother pushed me to pick a wedding gown, china, and silverware, and participate in all the other rituals getting married can entail. This included bridal showers where I'd open gifts and find insincere comments pouring out of my mouth like: "Oh, such and so, I've always wanted a set of Jell-O molds." It was worth it, however, because when the wedding was over with the ceremony and reception held at my father's synagogue—I would get to be with Nolan full-time. Our first time alone as a newly married couple was on our honeymoon as we journeyed down the California Pacific Coast Highway from San Francisco to Los Angeles.

I went from my parents' house to setting up house with him. I didn't know how to cook but learned by testing recipes from the cadre of cookbooks I received as shower and wedding gifts, such as *The I Hate to Cook Book*, where I learned to make speedballs, a conglomerate of ingredients—such as Lipton Onion Soup—that mimicked a meatball.

Nolan taught me how to drive a stick-shift car after trading in my two-year-old Karmann Ghia for a 1965 Mercedes 230SL that had blown a rod; he had it rebuilt. We'd take long drives on weekends in the car I nicknamed "Nellie." We were a good pair. We'd put the top down and laugh and talk and get sunburned driving Nellie to garage and estate sales to ferret out much needed furniture to fill our first apartment— furniture that we'd fix, sand, restain, or paint. Some of my greatest treasures, such as our burled wood, refectory, dining room table and chairs, were bought at bargain basement prices in those days.

Our early years were a bit glamorous at times, too: He was in the music business for a large record company. When we weren't hanging out with friends or engaged in such projects as gardening, painting furniture, and staining hardwood floors or wallpapering a room, our weekends were often spent at concerts rubbing elbows with rising musical stars like Helen Reddy, Linda Ronstadt, Glen Campbell, and even the Beatles. Although less exciting, I had just gotten my first writing job for a major local shoe company. I loved the work and amassed the best shoe collection of anyone I knew. I left to attend graduate school, but didn't finish when offered a job writing for a Jewish community newspaper where I interviewed such giants as David Ben-Gurion and Elie Wiesel. I was sent on a press junket to Israel and Vienna, Austria, where we visited Mauthausen-Gusen concentration camp. The images I saw haunted me for years and had a profound effect on my life. I read all I could about the Holocaust and even taught a course to eighth graders.

During those early marital years, we were frugal, agreeing to live only on my husband's salary and sock away mine. We were pioneers: Everything we learned about marriage, we experienced together as we moved several times from the affordable first apartment in our hometown to our first small but charming, suburban, brick, colonial-style home with a large, fenced yard. We saw this as a good investment, and it was. A transfer to Chicago meant we had to sell our home, which we did for a profit. We moved to a vintage city apartment with hardwood floors and high ceilings.

Each of us had our jobs, and in Chicago we made a new circle of friends, who became like family. We worked long hours, Nolan traveled a lot during the week and when home we visited the city's many fabulous museums, ate in many of Chicago's inexpensive restaurants in the developing Near North Side where we lived, walked our dog, rode our bicycle built for two along Lake Shore Drive, traveled to New England and Europe, and one year attended the Grammy Awards held in Nashville, Tennessee. Then, before the arrival of our first child, we bought a home in a northern suburb. A year later, when my husband was offered another promotion and a transfer to Southern California, he opted instead to go into my family's wholesale wine and spirits business, and so we returned home. We agreed it would be a healthier environment to raise our then only child, who would be surrounded by grandparents, aunts, uncles, and cousins.

I'll never forget that first day he stepped into our family business to work with my father. I had continued to work in Chicago for a magazine after our son was born, but I decided to stay home and freelance after our move back home. Nolan suggested the topic of one of the first articles I sold. He had received a copy of a fledgling magazine called *Inc.* "Why not write a family business story for the magazine?" he suggested. This led to the first book Barbara and I coauthored about family businesses. Published in 1989, it resulted in a close friendship and partnership that has lasted more than 30 years.

For forty-two years, despite the ups and downs or maybe because of them, Nolan and I had a good life. We believed in the same values and felt that differences could be talked about and fixed—or at least argued fairly—most of the time. Naturally, there were heated disagreements and yelling, mostly about our kids—where they should go to school or how to discipline them for being disrespectful or disobeying a rule such as driving the car when they were told they could not. We had different parenting styles. He was indulgent but had a hair-trigger temper. I was slightly tougher but inconsistent in doling out punishment. Our disagreements would crescendo and then slowly decrescendo when Nolan would flash his smile and use charm to tease, joke, and make fun of the situation without harming our relationship irrevocably. In retrospect, I've learned to believe what F. Scott Fitzgerald wrote in *This Side of Paradise*: "Very few things matter and nothing matters very much."

The high points in our lives and our marriage were many: the births of our three children, their successes in school and in work; job promotions and awards; my 10 years as a first soprano with the Bach Society;

my husband's jam sessions and occasional gigs on weekends; birthday and anniversary celebrations; large family gatherings and trips to the beach; classes we took together; jobs we volunteered for such as helping at the Red Cross during a major flood in 1993; excursions for his wine and spirits distributing job, which included a sherry festival in Spain, a distillery trip to Scotland, a beer junket to Switzerland, and so much more. We also shared some sad moments, like the death of his father, a young first cousin, our various dogs, and my maternal grandparents.

The lovely thing about marriage is that life ambles along a path lined with security and direction—until something throws it wildly off course. Neither of us was prepared to hear "cancer" after a visit to a doctor. Neither of us could have imagined that Nolan would have to fight illness for five long years that ended his life way too soon.

BARBARA

MY STORY

During the second semester of my junior year in college, in 1970, I decided at the last minute to accompany my roommate to a regular university-sponsored mixer on a Saturday night, attended mostly by guys in law or business school. Few women had matriculated at these graduate schools at the time.

My roommate and I sat opposite one another in a booth and waited for someone to come over and show interest in each of us, maybe even ask us to dance. I remember—forty-five years later—that I wore tie-dyed purple, blue, and white pants and a white top, my take on a bohemian-style uniform that reflected I was an undergrad at a liberal women's college in New York City during the Vietnam era.

It was there I met my future husband, a "one L," or first-year student. He sauntered over in a preppy, law-school uniform of chinos, long-sleeved checked shirt, and Weejuns-style loafers. His looks definitely appealed to me with his full head of dark curly hair, slender build, and quiet demeanor. He asked if he could join us. I think I probably smiled. I know I said, "Yes," and he sat down next to me. We had no problem conversing, originally about "schlock art," which referenced the Yiddish term for shoddy, cheap works.

He walked me back to the apartment where I was living, and said he would call. At exactly 10:15 p.m., after the law school library closed the next Monday night, he did. He asked me out for our first date, for the next Saturday night. We went to a restaurant in cool, hip downtown Greenwich Village. I remember kissing him on that date. I don't remember if anybody was around, and frankly did not care. It seemed incredibly gutsy, given my prudish upbringing, and I was thrilled.

After another week of more late-evening calls, we went on our second date to see a French thriller, *Rider on the Rain*. I still recall its frightening plot. There was another date soon for which I cooked dinner in the college dorm suite I had moved into. I remember consulting one suite mate and asking her to help plan a romantic feast. I made what seemed exotic back then: shish kabob skewers of chunks of beef laced with colorful vegetables, rice, and ambrosia for dessert, a fruit salad with shredded coconut that was said to be an elixir. After that meal, he showed sufficient interest in me that I began to feel secure and stopped counting our dates.

I was still dating others, and think he was, too, but at some point we developed a routine of what then was sweetly called courtship—weekend dates on most Fridays and Saturdays, the big date nights at the time, and sometimes seeing one another for lunch or studying during the week. Of course, my now thirty-something daughters would consider our courtship as archaic as the formal rituals of how men pursue women on *Downton Abbey*. It seems old fashioned to me now, too, but the bottom line was the same regardless of era or evolving social mores: the expectation that if a relationship had legs, it would end in marriage.

Nobody I knew lived together back then; we stayed overnight for sure, but we were secretive about such goings-on, hiding our diaphragms and birth-control pills from our parents, and making excuses for our absences when they called, since there only were landlines. I didn't care. I was having great fun, and I liked that my boyfriend was smart, cute, had a sense of humor, was ambitious in a healthy way, and shared similar values and religion, which was important to both of us at the time and to our parents. He also was eager to learn to play tennis with me, meet my friends, and spend time together. I was eager to learn about his law studies and hear about his college fencing and interest in photography.

I never experienced the lightning bolt that Margaret felt, and I never asked if he did, either. We also had some cultural differences due to family backgrounds. My parents had been born in this country. His had emigrated from Germany during World War II. Yet, I believed any differences would matter far less as we spent more time together. The steadiness and stability of our deepening relationship seemed strong enough glue for a lifetime together.

After all, I had gone off to college in fall 1967 with the goals of doing well academically, deciding on a profession, and finding a potential spouse by the time I graduated with a BA. Those messages had been drummed into me loudly by my traditional parents.

My parents believed, and I knew, too, that college offered the best place to meet an appropriate mate. Having a career of my own was wise, but it would never be as important as my husband's. I was going for the diamond solitaire. He would get the brass ring and climb his way up the corporate ladder.

Times were slowly changing. Many of the women I met once I transferred to a women's college in New York City were making me rethink exactly how I would balance my goals. My new classmates seemed much more determined to enter male-dominated professions and also have families, though marriage immediately was not a goal. There also wasn't talk yet of glass ceilings, since so few women had gained positions in companies, firms, and academia where they might break through.

After I met my future husband, when I debated spending the summer studying painting and printmaking at an upstate New York university or in Los Angeles, he urged me to stay closer to Manhattan so we could see one another on weekends. That seemed a bigger sign of commitment than our regular weekend dates.

I went to the upstate school, a five-hour bus ride away, and we kept in touch with calls, letters, and visits. We continued our relationship into the fall and soon hit milestones: our first Chanukah together (he gave me Julia Child's *Mastering the Art of French Cooking* with a sweet poem inscribed); New Year's Eve with friends and family; my twenty-second birthday dinner at a family member's apartment with fresh steamed lobsters, and then the anniversary of our first year dating.

Our relationship continued to be comfortable and full. He made me feel good about myself. We dove head first into each other's interests. He took a course in art history; I took a course for undergraduates about law and even considered (for one night, at his urging), taking the LSATs to go to law school. (By the next morning, I had come to my senses.) We toasted each other's accomplishments when he secured a summer law firm job in a difficult market, and I got into a Master's program to study art history and painting.

And we did what I hoped would happen. More than a year after dating we started talking about marriage, as some of our friends also did. We decided we'd wait until he graduated law school and was working full-time. But we were encouraged by my father, who believed in the institution, to move up the timetable. "Why wait?" he asked. "You can manage it financially." In retrospect, I believe he wanted me off his payroll and wasn't going to support me by paying rent for an off-campus apartment and graduate tuition. He thought my husband could swing it since I would now be his chattel. My mother helped on the sly with my modest tuition.

We married in fall 1971, four months after I graduated. He was twenty-three. I was twenty-two. We were babies, and to this day, his photo in the wedding album—wearing a black tuxedo with black bow tie, formal white shirt, and black patent leather shoes—looks like it could have been from his Bar Mitzvah.

We managed financially with summer jobs and wedding savings, a part-time job he had wanted at his undergraduate college, and modest expectations regarding our wardrobes, entertainment, transportation, and food choices. We took subways and buses rather than buy our own car, as friends had. At home, we dined inexpensively on Mrs. Pawl's frozen fish sticks and Chef Boyardee canned ravioli. But we lived nicely in a furnished, one-bedroom, rent-stabilized New York City apartment rather than in a law school dorm.

Once we graduated and started working, in 1972, we had what we considered a staggering income of $22,000—$16,000 from his job at a large Wall Street law firm and $6,000 for mine at a national design magazine where we were told, "If you need more money, go ask Mommy or Daddy." We thought we had hit the jackpot. We were able to save most of my salary, go to movies and theater, where we saw Meryl Streep's stage debut, enjoy one big vacation a year—along California's coast, to France, England, Hawaii—entertain, and purchase a small charming suburban house four years after marrying.

More important, we had forged a partnership long before the expression "having each other's backs" became a cliché. We each worked hard at our careers. He helped me get through accounting when I started work on my next graduate degree, a Masters in Business Administration, an MBA, as I saw more newspapers start special business sections. I envisioned myself segueing from writing about design to reporting on financial news. He also read and edited most of my articles; I trusted his objectivity and smarts. I read his legal writings, which I barely understood but was impressed with, as his writing became crisper and clearer with help from a law firm mentor.

We went out together alone on many Friday evenings after he emerged from endless hours at work during the week, sometimes in the wee hours with a few hours to sleep a bit, shower, change, and head back to the office. We never had a problem talking or finding things we loved doing together—walking around our neighborhood, learning about wine, discovering American antiques, trying recipes together. He helped me roll a Buche de Noel one holiday, and together we perfected a Caesar salad recipe a law school classmate shared. He took charge of coddling the eggs and mincing anchovies; I sautéed bread for fresh croutons. When he was at work late in the evening, I kept busy with female friends in similar situations, took on extra work, which led to a first book inspired by Amish quilts, and continued my MBA coursework. Saturdays were reserved usually for friends, and we worked in family obligations.

Only eventually—after eight years of marriage, friends starting to become parents, and more direct comments from wannabe grandparents—did we decide we were ready to try to have a baby. Month after month it didn't happen. We started down the painful path of infertility—a specialist, sperm counts, hormone level checks, preplanned calendar intimacy, and then shots, pills, and surgery for me.

At the same time, we continued to enjoy a steady life we never questioned. We focused on my husband's making partner, on having a child together, on developing my journalism career, which I might scale back or do part-time some day if we had kids, and living in the city until we relocated to the suburbs. But when the local job market proved disappointing, we took the first gutsy step to chart our own adult course.

He placed an ad in a legal publication, looking for a challenging opportunity. Interest came from a top midwestern firm. I couldn't imagine leaving our Eastern roots until the possibility became reality with an offer. Neither could many of our provincial New York friends. They were shocked. "Where are you going?" "Why?" "Is there anything to do there besides go to baseball games?" We headed off on a three-week romantic vacation in France, promising not to weigh pros and cons until we returned. Before the trip was over and we had eaten our last bites of fabulous quenelles, he sent a postcard to friends, hinting at the idea.

I worried about giving up a job I loved and moving to a family-oriented city without the guarantee of children, my own or adopted. As a team, we decided to relocate for his job if I found one and my fertility problems seemed solvable. When I got a part-time offer from the consumer news section at the city's main daily newspaper, acceptance into an MBA program on a part-time basis, and an appointment with the top fertility expert in our new city, the stars seemed aligned. It was time to go, even though leaving our families and friends proved difficult. Yet, it felt like a grown-up, healthy, and even slightly courageous decision. We headed west.

Initially, all boded well. An infertility doctor prescribed a different treatment; I became pregnant the first month, miscarried, and then pregnant again several months later with our first daughter. I loved the hubbub of a newsroom, was offered full-time employment, and continued work on my MBA. Soon it became too difficult with one, then two young daughters. I gave up finishing my MBA. Seven years later, I also took a leave of absence to start work on a family business book with Margaret, after a mutual friend introduced us.

Life seemed rosy. My husband made partner, wrote legal articles, joined legal groups, attended meetings, ran, made friends. We bought a wonderful 1929 brick house on a great block with pink sidewalks where he taught our older daughter to ride a bike without training wheels, the neighbors cheering her on. He planted tulips one spring in a huge circle before our second daughter arrived. We entertained stylishly in our red lacquered dining room, mixing people together like an eclectic musical program. We planned trips, collected furniture and folk art, saved money, and both of us seemed happy with the slower pace. We also relished the richer social life than we had experienced in New York. Our adopted city was known for being tough on allowing nonnatives to break

into its tight circles—often three generations knowing each other intimately. Yet we were able to, in part, because I had an aunt and uncle
living there who were popular, because of our work contacts, and because it was so unusual for two young native New Yorkers to give the
city a try. We instinctively sensed the importance of reciprocating
whenever invited and not criticizing how different life was in the Heartland.

When I look back on those years to try to trace the first bread
crumbs that might explain the eventual failure of our marriage, I see
few. We were a good partnership. We enjoyed many similar interests
and raising two young daughters. We made key decisions together. We
weathered personal and job hurdles, disappointments, disagreements,
illnesses, and deaths, and eventually decided to move again eight years
after arriving. A prestigious opportunity emerged for him through a law
school classmate, and he was eager to accept. I had serious doubts
about the next firm's culture and his colleagues' very different backgrounds. I verbalized my concerns, but he was excited about the offer. I
clearly remember him saying, "I have to take it." How could I argue
with such determination? Moreover, I know I loved him. I thought he
loved me, and remember friends telling me he acted and spoke like I
walked on water. I felt we were there for each other as husbands and
wives are expected to be.

Those years seemed so promising and happy, a foreboding of more
good things to come. Until one day, close to twenty-nine years after we
married, he told me he had never been happy. I honestly never knew.

LOVE STRUCK SECOND TIME AROUND

People wonder; can you find real passion when you're older, decades
after your lusting teen years? Absolutely. Dorothy P. met the love of her
life but not until she admitted to herself how unhappy she was in her
first marriage. The timing wasn't exactly ideal and almost a cliché. She
and her high school boyfriend, each married, both attended their
30th reunion without their spouses and not knowing the other would be
there. "When I walked into the room and saw Bryan G., that lightning
bolt hit. The fact we both were married didn't seem to matter. His
marriage was dead. When I was honest with myself, mine was, too. I

knew that my husband was having a long-time affair. He had told me and thought we could still stay married. He viewed it as a deal. Because my life was filled with running a company, civic interests, and raising children, I didn't have the energy to deal with a resolution. Rather, I put my marriage on the back burner," says Dorothy.

Back in the late 1960s, Dorothy had gone out with Bryan several times during their last year in high school and over the summer. Dorothy's very traditional Jewish father wasn't happy, however. To him, their different religions were like nails on a blackboard. Every time Dorothy came home from a date with Bryan, her dad waited in their living room with arms crossed and an angry scowl on his face. He tried to fix her up with nice Jewish young men. Nothing took.

Natural consequences stepped in. Dorothy and Bryan went off to different colleges, 2,000 miles apart. Dorothy also knew a long-distance relationship would never work. Once she matriculated at college, she had no thoughts of seeing Bryan again, until he invited her to his freshman homecoming. Her feelings were fueled again. Because an older brother lived in the same city, her father agreed to let her go, knowing that his son would be a dutiful chaperone. The romantic relationship barely progressed, and when Bryan came to visit Dorothy without her permission, she refused to see him.

Two weeks after her first date with someone Jewish who had a good job and seemed amiable, she was engaged at 21; her fiancée was 26. Though he was Jewish, her father never warmed to him and whispered to her as he walked her down the aisle, "It doesn't matter that there is a roomful of people. You can still bow out if you have any doubts," she says, recalling her response, "I'm good; we're good. Don't worry." She went through with the marriage, had two sons, pursued a successful career in her family's business, eventually sold it to a huge conglomerate, but treaded water throughout the marriage. "The passion was never there. I never completely forgot Bryan, even though we never slept together."

At Dorothy's high school reunion in October 1998, the two were inseparable the entire evening and ended up spending the night together. Bryan insisted that if they would pursue a relationship, it wasn't going to be clandestine. Each asked for a divorce. Less than a year later, each was single, and with her sons grown and on their own, Dorothy moved 2,000 miles west to where Bryan lived. Many of her friends told her she was insane. "Everybody had advice, except for my mom who was for it. But she always bucked trends." Slightly more than another year later, in July 1999, they married.

More than sixteen years later, Dorothy says with confidence she has no regrets that she made the right decision the second time around. "It's never too late to find real love and passion. Of course, I was only forty-nine, which is a big difference from now being sixty-five when many seek companionship and respect more than physical intimacy. For once, I went with my gut. I'm a secular Jew, so the religious difference didn't matter, and Bryan isn't religious at all. The early years were challenging because of the adjustments—new city, new job, new friends, parenting four kids. But we followed our tsunami of emotions and the physical magnetism. Most of all, we were determined to make our marriage work."

All the angst has now disappeared, and they're proud of their relationship, coping with four grown children, illnesses, and various stages of aging. "He's my best friend and lover. I'd tell others if you find that special person, go for it. You don't get many chances at real love."

2

HELL ABOVE GROUND

MARGARET

LOSING A LOVE

It was a freezing November morning as we pulled into the hospital parking garage. My husband was indefatigably cheerful. I was morose. You'd think it would be the reverse. He was the one having a CAT scan and biopsy to see if the dramatic rise in his PSA level, a prostate-specific antigen test done through blood analysis, indicated prostate cancer.

And then we went home and waited for the results. Two days later, while looking at a collection of modern European paintings at our area's main art museum, my husband's cell phone rang. He stepped away from me, walked into a corridor, and listened. The biopsy for prostate cancer was positive and, by the way, the scan showed a mass of lymphoma cells in his bladder. With that one phone call, the start of our five-year-battle with cancer began.

Radioactive seeds were inserted to cure the prostate cancer. More scans and blood tests showed the lymphoma was isolated in his bladder. Seventeen days of radiation was given to him over a four-week period to zap the lymphoma cells. The radiologist/oncologist recommended that my husband follow up with a lymphoma specialist/oncologist. He was lucky to get in to see the top lymphoma doctor at our local cancer center and checked out fine. "See you in six months," the doctor said optimistically. All seemed under control. Nolan had minimal discomfort.

Six months later my husband went for the checkup, and the lymphoma specialist felt a lump under one arm. "And there's a twin under the other arm," she said. "What is she talking about?" I thought. I began to fire questions in my reportorial fashion: "What does this mean?" Before the doctor could answer, I asked, "Does he have lymphoma in other places?"

"I don't know," she said.

Tests were recommended—a biopsy of an enlarged lymph node in his left arm pit confirmed the diagnosis of marginal zone B-cell non-Hodgkin's lymphoma. A PET scan (positron emission tomography) was ordered to pinpoint what areas of the body were involved.

Initially, we had to make choices about each diagnosis and subsequent treatment. Our parents told us to do whatever doctors recommended. They were part of a generation that believed everything doctors told them. Not us.

My husband and I agreed to become partners to fight this insidious disease. Dig. Ask questions. Go to the right sources—books, tapes, videos, websites, doctors who knew other doctors, second opinions, the newest treatments, and even clinical trials. We learned there is a right and wrong way to talk to doctors. Don't tiptoe around issues. Have a list of tough questions and either video, tape record, or write the information down. Check and double check. Don't go to appointments alone. You need a second pair of ears. Most important, question everything whether it's the right drug and dose, right treatment, and right treatment center. Mistakes, we learned, can be made because of carelessness, poor preparation, limited staff, and too many patients. Refuse treatment if you're sure the shot or pill isn't right, which happened a few times. Make sure the nurse administers everything correctly. Be sure you have good insurance, which we fortunately did. If not, see if you can tap family and friends for the funds, or organize a grassroots fundraiser, or do it online.

We questioned all. Should we go elsewhere for a second opinion? Yes, our oncologist said. She sent his records to two major cancer centers for review. Both oncologists at those centers concurred that the diagnosis and treatment were the same they'd recommend. We had enough information to move forward. There was every reason to think my husband would be fine.

He received the first infusion of chemotherapy at the cancer center in our hometown. We walked onto the floor that contained a series of small treatment rooms called "pods." There was a flurry of activity in the pod as people filed in for their infusions and left. Some had no hair, a visible sign they were having chemo; some women wore scarves or wigs; some patients were very sick and wheeled in, while others appeared healthy. They might be in the early stages of their chemo, on a chemo regimen that didn't cause hair loss, or there for another reason, such as a bone medicine infusion. The nurses were diligent, checking and rechecking the bags of chemicals to make sure they were correct and for the right patient. They hooked my husband up and started a very slow drip to test his reaction. This first infusion went on for hours. And for the next two months, every other week, this was his routine. He toughed it out, tolerating infusions of a toxic cocktail called R-CHOP, which combines rituximab, cyclophosphamide, doxorubicin, vincristine, and prednisone, all of which caused his thick, wavy dark hair to fall out.

Losing his hair everywhere, including his eyebrows, was the one consequence of the chemo that upset him the most; it was a visible sign of his illness. We quickly went to buy him a wig, though initially he refused to leave the house. In addition to mild nausea and some loss of taste, he had one infection that was controlled with IV antibiotics that had to be administered in the hospital.

A couple months and three cycles of R-CHOP later, he had a bone marrow biopsy and CAT scan, which indicated he was in remission. That evening we opened a bottle of Dom Perignon my husband had saved for a special occasion, such as a child's wedding or birth of a grandchild. We didn't expect to be toasting to good health. We also were too naïve at this time to think that our journey with cancer might not be ended.

Shortly after, our lives went back to a normal routine: work for both of us, making dates with friends, though my husband would tire easily; a trip to New York to visit one of our kids; family dinners for holidays and special events; Nolan mowing the lawn, cleaning the gutters, barbecuing, taking our dog for walks, biking, going to concerts. We each had little interest in sex; our intimacy had descended to a new level. Holding hands and occasional snuggling seemed more meaningful.

But cancer is a lifetime disease. After almost a year, I knew something wasn't right with his health. He would clump up the stairs breathing heavily. "I'm fine," he'd say and shoo me away when I asked what was happening. Back to the doctor for a checkup and bone marrow biopsy revealed the lymphoma had returned. More chemo, more hair loss, more nausea, more pills and infections, and more bone marrow tests and CAT and PET scans.

My husband was emphatic: Do not discuss the illness with anyone, including our parents and children. We only told them the basics and characterized everything he was going through as good news. "He's weak but getting stronger, which means he's healing." Not only was he a very private person who despised being thought of as sick, but he also didn't want to worry anyone and wanted to keep working. I confided little in my siblings for the same reason.

I was feeling alone and needed to vent. I did the research online to find a local family caregiver, cancer support group.

One freezing winter night I entered a tiny room with dim lighting. Chairs and some well-worn sofas lined the room as people—some in business attire and others in jeans and T-shirts—weaved around a coffee table, hoping to meet other family caregivers in similar situations. I'd spend two hours a week there discussing and learning about how to live and battle cancer and acquiring a new vocabulary: neutrophils, autologous, Neupogen.

The problems of those in the group covered an enormous range. I listened raptly to the stories these strangers spewed as if it were oxygen I needed to breathe. There was a young pregnant woman with a brown ponytail who teared up while telling how she was taking care of her mother whose breast cancer had returned and who might not live to see her first grandchild. An elderly man who seemed to be the most pragmatic and experienced in the group—his wife had been fighting her cancer for 12 years and now was dying—recommended books and articles. He counseled those of us in the group to get our finances in order or write a will just in case. One woman in her 40s had a spouse with multiple melanomas, which had metastasized to his lungs. They had hit the financial wall with their insurance company. Do we mortgage our home? There was a clinical trial they could try at MD Anderson Cancer Center in Texas, a premier treatment hospital. Another woman in her mid-60s, head of a nonprofit agency, was caring for a life partner with a brain tumor. There was little hope. A forty-something man described his wife's stage-four colon cancer that had metastasized to her liver. It was discovered during a routine colonoscopy. They had four kids under age twelve. The prognosis was grim.

It's because of these people in this safe place that I found comfort, a chance to listen to the stories of others and voice my concerns. And when my husband went back to the hospital for another round of chemotherapy, I was in a better place emotionally. We both knew the drill. Again, he went into remission, and was placed on a maintenance drug called Rituxan.

Then months later again I knew something was awry. Many days I'd come home from work—he worked from home at that time, doing movie advertising—and he'd be sleeping on his lazy boy chair near the bedroom window. I'd ask him what was going on. He wouldn't answer. Should I talk and ask questions or keep my mouth shut? This was tough for me to do. How do I bring up my concerns? I wanted him to talk about his illness with me and open up about how he felt. He continued to try to hide his sickness.

One morning he woke with a high fever, I ran to the phone to call the hospital, and he yelled, "No. Stop." I screamed out of frustration. "Your doctor said to call her if your temperature goes above 101 degrees." He relented after we exchanged harsh words. I helped him dress and walk to the car, and we rushed to the hospital. His red blood count was dangerously low. He went on IV antibiotics, the fever dropped, and he came home. When I talked about this in the support group, many suggested that I take care of what I could control: go to work, continue my freelance writing, spend time with friends, exercise, eat healthy, try to sleep well. I also continued to research—talking to others who had dealt with cancer and going online or to the library to seek out the latest, best treatments. I was adamant that cancer wasn't going to define my life. Why should it? Nolan would eventually go into remission or be cured. It would just take time.

I continued to remain optimistic. I had to be, even though he wasn't getting better and was tired all the time. His red blood counts began to undulate. It was back to the hospital for more tests. A bone marrow test spotted some large B-cell lymphoma cells. Aggressive. Fast spreading.

More tests. More treatments. Recommendation: an autologous stem cell transplant, which meant he'd be his own donor. And thus the journey to stay alive and eradicate the cancer was stepped up. We had to fill out dozens of forms, including a psychological profile that would verify my husband and I were strong enough emotionally and in our marriage to endure the next leg of this saga. Also more medical tests. Was his heart strong enough? His kidneys? After going through a few days of what's called "pheresis" to isolate hundreds of thousands of his stem cells, he was ready to have them transplanted to boost his immune system.

Day one. We drove to the hospital; it was mid-February 2010. Nolan was assigned to a special floor and a private room for patients receiving stem cell transplants. A woman in purple sweats and a smock covered with smiling Disney characters greeted us. She was all chitchat and friendliness as we followed her to a private room where my husband would fight for his life for the next four weeks. It started with "conditioning chemotherapy," strong chemotherapy before the transplant, to eradicate all cancer cells. I was told that roughly 50 percent of aggressive lymphomas are cured with autologous stem cell transplantation. This caused stomach issues and horrific nausea. But he could endure it, we reasoned, for this was what we hoped would be the dénouement to an almost four-year struggle.

He came home, his body thin and vulnerable, with fragile and irregular breathing. He had a thicker, hacking cough. I thought: What next? Although I was working full-time, coping with his increasing physical needs was manageable, but exhausting. I was cleaning his port, now the conduit for his chemo drugs and blood transfusions, taking his temperature when he'd let me, preparing special foods he could ingest such as oatmeal, soft-boiled eggs, or chicken soup with rice. I'd run home from work at noon to check on him and let the dog out. I asked a neighbor across the street to keep an eye on him. I'd leave the back door open. I tried to think of ways to pep things up. I would search for a spot of humor, a story, gossip, anything to make him laugh—a little levity. He started to teach me how to play chess. We played gin and Scrabble. We watched endless hours of old movies, mostly comedies like the Marx Brothers or Abbott and Costello, on our new, huge, flat-screen TV my husband had wanted. Our kids signed us up for Netflix.

He finally got strong enough to go back to work. Fortunately, he could still do most of it from home. I saw this as a positive step and convinced myself that he was on his way to beating cancer. But as I continued my routine of going to work, coming home and doing what I could for my husband, I was wearing down. I felt drained and crabby. Work became tough for me. I would start projects I couldn't finish, and picked fights with my sisters or my boss. I felt guilty leaving Nolan alone all day. Should I quit and be with him?

That's when I found a therapist who helped me find strategies to cope: Take care of myself: exercise—I'd walk on my treadmill in our basement every morning before work; sleep—I'd take melatonin to help when I'd get up several times each night to see if Nolan was still breathing; drink no coffee after 3 p.m., no sugar after an early dinner; continue to arm myself with information—I'd spend hours on the Internet looking up treatments and hoping to find success stories; get out of the house when I could—meeting friends for wine or an early dinner or doing a volunteer project with kids in a public clinic on Saturday mornings to get outside myself; and keep working. When I was at my job or busy with a project I didn't focus on what I was facing at home.

And then there were a few bright spots. When Nolan became ill, our eldest son moved back home for a new job and was the most attentive I'd ever seen. "Here dad, let me hold the pan (for nausea). Let me walk you to the bathroom. What can I get you?" When my husband drove himself to the hospital one morning for tests and was too sick to drive home, our son left work to pick him up. Or there was the night we attended a survivor's dinner. It was a badge of honor to have survived the stem cell treatment, tangible proof of his courage and strength. He was doing pretty well at that point. Saturday nights out with friends, Sundays with the newspaper and doughnuts, trips to the art museum and concerts, walks in the park with our wheaten terrier. We made plans, although many nights we had to cancel at the last moment.

Many people were there for us every moment. Barbara, in whom I confided, stood by us unconditionally. She had survived divorce. She listened and held my hand. So did my best childhood friend and her husband. He had survived bone cancer. My boss and coworkers, with whom I also had to share information, were wonderful, asking what they could do. I would get cards and food. One coworker made us challah. A group of girlfriends from high school sent us a gigantic basket of goodies. Friends cooked and brought over lunches and dinners. My parents took me to dinner and brought us food. My sisters who live out of town would send our favorite treats. My brother-in-law, married to my husband's sister, walked our dog.

Another high point was an invitation from a prominent businessman and his wife, friends of our eldest son, who invited us to sit in their luxury box at the opening game of the 2010 Cardinals baseball season. Although tired, there was no way Nolan would miss this opportunity.

That winter, he insisted we take a trip to Los Angeles to see our daughter and her new apartment. We went to the doctor together who said it was fine. We left for a week. He was fine on the plane and for the first two days, and then began to fade. He didn't want to walk or go to a museum with us, he didn't care about dinner. He tried a few times to rally because he didn't want our daughter to see him this way. I barely got him on the plane to come home, and once back, after he finally made it up the stairs, he collapsed into bed.

He grew weaker. Breathing more labored. A few weeks later I said, "Please, call the doctor and schedule a checkup. Just humor me." Every checkup started with a blood test to show his counts. We waited for the results. His doctor came in and said she wasn't happy with his numbers. "How was he feeling?" she asked. "You look well."

My husband said he felt fine. I was furious that he couldn't even be candid with his doctor so I chimed in, "Do you really want to know what a day in the life is like living with Nolan Crane right now? He is in bed all day; he can barely make it up the stairs, and rarely even goes downstairs now. He's eating nothing." She turned to my husband and said without hesitation, "I want you to have a bone marrow biopsy right now."

We went home and once again waited and waited for the results. Usually, when the news was bad, we'd hear pretty quickly. Waiting this long we thought was a good sign. But it was taking too long so one morning from work I called his doctor to find out what was happening. She sounded more serious than usual. "Meg, go home I want to talk to both of you." Shaking, I raced out the door, jumped in my car and made it home in record time. I ran upstairs, quickly called the doctor and put Nolan on the other line. The news was terrible: Nolan's illness had morphed into something called, "myelodysplastic syndrome," which I learned later was incurable. "What's next?" Nolan asked. She suggested he consider another stem cell transplant with a donor or try a new chemo drug for this condition—a drug that would prolong his life a year or two. I still was in denial about the fact that he might not live.

We made an appointment to discuss options with his doctor. "Here's the situation," she said. "If you opt for the stem cell transplant, you'll only have a 40 percent chance of living through it." He chose to try the new chemo drug Azacitidine that turned out to be the most toxic of all. After the third of five infusions, the doctor stopped treatment, although my husband fought her decision. Another bone marrow biopsy showed that at least the three infusions had done some good.

And then one beautiful and peaceful spring morning a few weeks later, with the flowers just starting to bloom and the sun blazing, my husband got up to go to the bathroom and passed out on the floor. Our youngest son had just come home to visit. He came rushing in and was able to pick his father up and put him in a chair. Nolan's fever was soaring and I told him I was calling an ambulance. Stoic as usual, he dismissed the idea, worrying about what the neighbors would think. He asked me to help him get dressed, so I could drive him to the hospital. When he got up to put on his jeans, he passed out again. I immediately called 911.

The paramedics put him on a gurney and rushed him to the hospital. Four weeks later, he was still in the hospital. His breathing was getting weaker and took most of his energy. He ate almost nothing and lost all control over bodily functions. Feverish, irritable, he still struggled for breath. Oxygen was administered. He was given massive doses of Ativan to make him comfortable. The hospital gave him daily blood transfusions and pain meds as needed. People sent cards. Our rabbi offered prayers. Some nights, when he still had an appetite, we brought in his favorite foods: Imo's Pizza and White Castle, pastrami sandwiches from a nearby deli. I also knew at that point, I would have to start relying on more family support to give me relief. My eldest son and I took turns sitting beside him. My mother-in-law, brother-in-law, sisters, and nieces visited him.

When I was in the parking lot at work one Friday morning in April, my cell rang. It was the doctor who said, "Every treatment had been tried and nothing is working. You might want to call your two children who live out of town and tell them to come home immediately." I remember thinking how would I ever track down our youngest son who is a musician and was on tour abroad in a small town in Spain. It took him two days to get home. Our daughter, who was out of town for a job interview in Napa Valley, California, when I contacted her, jumped on a plane and arrived home the next day. Although I was supposed to attend an event for work that night, I told my office I wouldn't be there and why, went straight home, and waited until my daughter's plane landed.

I never thought we'd lose him, even right before the end. How could I plan for this? We had planned for births, schools, house purchases, taxes, insurance, retirement—but not death. We so dreaded the thought of death that my husband and I never talked about it. We had wills, but I wasn't cosigned on certain bank accounts, investments, or car titles. We had never purchased cemetery plots. I had to do everything now in crisis mode at the last minute per my attorney's advice. While Nolan was in the hospital failing more each day, our attorney's paralegal would come with papers. I had to convince him to sign documents giving me power of attorney and change or add names on other papers. He could barely write yet he still fought me. He was determined not to die.

But he grew worse. He asked his oncologist if there were a clinical trial or another chemo drug he could try. "No," she replied sadly. He stopped eating and drinking. His kidneys started to shut down. We were urged to consider hospice. I begged him to allow me to do this and take him home. He was conscious enough, however, to realize that once on hospice at home, he couldn't receive the daily blood transfusions he needed. He refused to leave. His pulse wavered, his blood pressure started to sink, and temperature rose. He was put on morphine for pain and gradually slipped into a semiconscious state. When the nurses told me they suspected the end was near, I slept in his room in a chair.

And then on a dreary, rainy Tuesday morning in April, with our entire family surrounding him, he died five years after first being diagnosed. Nothing prepared me for the reality of his loss. I had never lost anyone I was really close to. My parents were both alive in their eighties and nineties; so were my siblings, and even Nolan's mother was doing well at age ninety-five. We had three healthy children. Now he was gone.

I had no idea what I was supposed to do. Grief paralyzed me. Do I call the funeral home, run out and buy a plot, cut a lock of his hair as a keepsake? Do I sit in the room with the corpse and wait until the funeral home comes to take the body away? I panicked. How do I put together a funeral much less a shiva? Nolan had always planned every major event with the right food, wine, and music. These were among the crazy thoughts and images whizzing through my mind at the dizzying speed of a slide show.

My children and I pulled together and talked about what to do next. My eldest son, who was used to being in charge, took over. "Mom, you call the funeral home and then people at your work to let them know." To his brother: "You contact your friends and their parents who knew Dad." To his sister: "You call all of mother's friends to break the news. I'll call the rabbi."

The hospital social worker finally tapped me on my shoulder and suggested that it was time to call the funeral home. The rabbi showed up at the hospital and told us what to do and to expect. Shortly after, the funeral director, who was a good friend, appeared and I knew what that meant. He was there to remove the body.

The next morning, still dazed, we piled into my son's car and drove to the funeral home where the director helped us make the arrangements. My father went with us because he had worked with my husband and loved him. He knew what to do. We were shown coffins in a showroom. It was macabre. What clothes do you want to bury him in? Decide about the eulogies? Do you want a graveside funeral? How many limos? Where do you want the shiva? Do you want the obit in the paper? Where will he be buried? And on and on. We didn't have cemetery plots so I had to shop for those, too, not exactly the kind of real estate I envisioned I'd be purchasing in my 60s when we had talked about retiring and downsizing. Two days later, to help him write the eulogy, the rabbi came to our home and asked dozens of questions as we ticked off the details of Nolan's too-short but very colorful life.

The day of the funeral was a blur. The sanctuary was filled. Apparently, each of our kids spoke about the father they loved, as did my brother-in-law. Then, as if someone were holding up gauze in front of my face to blur the picture, I vaguely remember standing at my front door as people streamed into my house for the shiva and going through the motions of thanking, kissing, and hugging. The only comic relief was that one man showed up whom nobody knew. We decided he must have heard that the food would be plentiful and good. Afterward, one sister stayed on two weeks to help and comfort me. I knew I had to keep busy, sorting out finances, planning, working in the yard, sweeping the patio, working, working. No time to think. If I slowed down I'd think and fall apart. Write notes. Take care of business. Write in my journal. Get the life insurance taken care of. Talk to my CPA, also to the attorney.

The reality of what happened slowly began to sink in. I'd get in the shower and sob. The same thing happened the first time after his death when I saw his handwriting or his number listed on my phone. I'd get in the car and cry so hard I couldn't see where I was going. I'd be in the grocery store, start crying, and rush out leaving my filled cart in the aisle. I'd go home and just stare at his clothes sitting untouched in the closet—his unfilled shoes positioned on the floor where he left them, his sweaters and shirts organized by color and season, a new shirt still in the box, and his vast collection of ties in various patterns and shades. I refused to move a thing for I was sure he'd be back.

Each song on the radio would remind me of him. There were the days I thought I saw my husband on the street. My heart jumped. He had come back. I would sob after and feel sad for days. Looking at my youngest son's smile, or my eldest son's eyes, or my daughter's gestures and sense of humor reminded me of him. I avoided certain restaurants, wines, movie theaters, and music venues. I had a hole in my heart that I couldn't fill; the sadness and guilt were devastating. Could I have done more? Better research? Different doctors? Different major cancer centers in other cities? We would have flown anywhere—and back.

The solitarily mind gets stuck on the pain of a lost love, like a needle on a turntable. I continued to cry incessantly. Every night I'd have a glass or two of wine, something I had never done alone before. Everything was an effort, even brushing my teeth. I would languish under my warm comforter, stay up all night watching Turner Classic Movies to escape, or read a mindless book—anything to keep my mind off my loss. I went back to work after two months. I was still inconsolable and remember one day driving down a highway and wishing someone would hit me head on. It would end the pain instantly.

I knew I needed professional help. Seven months after Nolan died, I saw a psychologist who suggested that I join a grief support group, which I did soon after. I also took training to become a tutor for elementary school kids who needed help with writing and reading. This was a much-needed diversion.

Other Timetables

Although I knew I couldn't get on with my life until I had fully grieved the loss of my husband, other women who have had spouses die move forward sooner, while still others remain mired in grief far longer than I did. At first, Robin W., who I met in the grief support group, just stared at the TV or went from room to room carrying around her late husband's ashes. After she found a grief counselor and, she says, more important, our grief support group, her depression began to lift. "A friend recommended me for a job because she thought it was a good idea I start getting out of the house more. I wasn't sure I could get through the interview without crying but I did and I got the job. It gave my self confidence a big boost! " It gave her a reason to get up each day, dress nicely, and focus on something other than her loss.

Joan S. stayed out of work for 12 weeks and wasn't sure if she could go back, after her husband died. While at work, she was functional, but after work she'd come home and sob. She found a therapist almost immediately, but didn't want to talk in front of a group. More than a year after her husband passed away, she finally joined a grief support group where she felt safe to tell her story. Mary B., whose husband died suddenly, found solace by going to church. The first year after Pat E.'s husband died, she made some impulsive decisions, such as selling her house. It took her two years to be able to start taking some classes in an effort to craft a new life.

Natalie S., whose husband committed suicide, used alcohol and time with men to dull her pain. She wasn't sleeping and finally went to a specialist. It took almost two years, but she started to take a healthier turn—stopped drinking to excess, started sleeping regular hours and met someone terrific who has given her life new meaning.

Months of counseling and the grief support group I joined proved to be my lifelines. I woke one morning almost two years after Nolan died and don't know why, but thought, "Enough. I have to get on with my life." I still had three children who needed me more than ever; so did my parents, and Nolan's mother. And I needed to live again, too.

BARBARA

GETTING DUMPED

I had experienced great sadness and heartache: miscarrying after two years of infertility treatments, losing a beloved father to Alzheimer's, and witnessing my mother's battle with cancer. Now I was experiencing new, deep, aching feelings on a similar scale after my husband left: shock, grief, rage, and unrelenting misery that saturated my every pore. I was not prepared for the three-year contested divorce process, horrific loss of funds, and personal feeling of sadness that ate through my body like a toxin and led to high blood pressure and my first panic attic.

After years of diligent saving for college, vacations, and homes, my divorce made money hemorrhage faster than water gushing from a burst pipe. Every time I turned around, there was another monthly bill from my attorneys in big thousand-dollar increments, or a request for another retainer to fund a forensic accountant, process server, or specialist to prep me for depositions, interrogatories, and trial, if we got to that point. Even though my husband had wanted the divorce and had a much larger salary, I was told I would have to bear costs, too, though not to the same degree. At one point, the charges added up to more than $100,000, and I freaked. When my lawyer told me his partners felt pressure due to my outstanding receivables, we agreed I'd pay my bill down $1,000 a month, yet it kept getting larger.

I also had meltdowns as I was drilled to prepare for depositions and taught to answer only succinctly—"yes" and "no" to such questions as: Were you ever intimate with anyone other than your husband? Did you use protection? I was advised not to get defensive or, worse, hostile when being questioned in a deposition or at trial. Example: "Do you take any medication for memory?" Answer: "No, I don't. I have a good memory." Question: "But you don't recall who you said this to?" Answer: "I didn't say I had said it. I said, maybe. I don't recall." And then when being reprimanded, told: "Let the record reflect that every question she has to answer she looks at her lawyer."

Giving brief and sometimes one-word answers were tough for a loquacious person and writer. How did I get to add in: I was 100 percent faithful during the marriage. I never flirted with anyone. I started to date only when I was dumped! I didn't understand the validity of those questions and particularly the issue of protection when I knew we were never going to be intimate again. We weren't doing a remake of the movie, *It's Complicated* when former husband and wife Meryl Streep and Alec Baldwin have a tryst to see if they can rekindle their romance.

Throughout the course of the separation and divorce, I had a crash course in divorce law, which I knew little about since my parents had been married almost fifty years and few of my friends and relatives had divorced. I learned how the system works.

The first important lesson was that when one person contacts a lawyer, that may rule out or "conflict out" the other's using someone from that same firm, at least for a certain period. There are a number of factors involved in determining whether the firm has been conflicted-out by the first contact, but it is a very real problem. In my case, the morning after I learned my husband planned to divorce me, I called friends for recommendations of the best divorce lawyers in town. When I called the first two on the list and mentioned our names, I learned he had already called them. When had he done his research, how long had he planned to leave me, and when did he make these calls? But that was only the beginning.

I asked friends for additional legal recommendations, checked credentials, made my list, found three who hadn't yet been called, and made appointments to interview them in person. I was also told that chemistry mattered, this was almost like dating since we would be spending so much time together. I dressed nicely, applied makeup, and remember walking to the first appointment. I must have given off the vibe "I'm available," because for the first time since married, I remember a nice-looking man about my age smiling and saying, "Hello." It seemed a good omen. I gave my long-winded spiel to the lawyer of what had occurred over the last year or so. I explained how concerned I was for my husband based on what seemed such out of the blue behavior that he would give up on us. I know I teared up—all lawyers and therapists have tissue boxes handy—and I said I didn't want a divorce, but wanted to save our marriage. I would even fight a divorce legally or stall it if I could. I was totally caught off guard by the lawyer's reaction, "You need to think of yourself now; stop thinking about him." I was shocked since I had been reared to be the good daughter, wife, and mother who put others first.

Once I made my lawyer choice and paid a retainer, I found myself managing a second career. I had to learn the legal system's peculiar method of charging for time incurred in tenths or quarters of an hour, and master terminology I had never heard before such as "discovery," and "interrogatories," and "depositions," even though I was a huge fan of TV's legal dramas. This, on the other hand, was reality TV, and I was the star in the hot seat, being asked:

- What had I purchased as gifts for my first beau who emerged almost 16 months after I separated? He got colorful, patterned socks, a personalized calendar, homemade brownies, hardly the expensive stuff the other side's lawyers envisioned.
- What had we done when the beau came to my house? Ate homemade cheesecake and drank wine.
- Why couldn't I find a higher-paying job after working for thirty years and loving what I did—even after all this time? I replied in some version of, "My type of publishing had never been lucrative. I'm not the female version of John Grisham with best-selling mysteries."
- Why couldn't my octogenarian mother support me? She lived on a fixed income.

Paying for my home expenses and basic lifestyle became tougher. Occasionally, I was at fault. After my husband moved out and rented an apartment and I saw the first bill, I screeched to a friend, "How can we possibly afford two homes?" She took the opposite strategy. How could I afford not to go shopping with her and make at least one revenge purchase for my emotional sanity? I still own that first pair of pointy, sexy black Manolo Blahnik heels, even though back then, as a single, I had few places to wear them.

But most expenditures were to maintain our house, my health, and our daughters' expenses. I was determined to keep our house as an anchor for the girls. One was still in high school and devastated by the separation; the other had entered her freshman year of college almost 1,000 miles away. I wanted her to be able to come home to her familiar childhood bedroom, blue and yellow wallpaper, comforter, and all. But the expenses ran on and on like questions at a deposition:

- Mortgage

- Burglar alarm
- Lawn and garden maintenance and snow removal services
- Tree trimming
- Gutter cleaning
- Pest control service
- Home and healthcare insurance
- Car expenses for my aging Honda with 130,000 miles
- Grocery store bills
- Children's tuitions and lessons
- Trips back East to visit my aging mom and college-age daughter

My freelance writing represented a nice secondary income but hardly was equivalent to a corporate attorney's. We had made the decision jointly for me to work from home after our second move to another city, and our shared desire to have quality time as a family.

When he moved out, I quickly found there often was no money at the end of each month. I clipped coupons that I used on days when grocery stores offered double and triple points; I rarely filled the car with a full tank of gasoline; I spread out appointments for hair cuts and colorings for roots so obvious no one questioned me when I said, "I'd like a senior ticket;" trimmed food expenses by turning to generic brands and learned to subsist on less; went to fewer movies and enjoyed more TV; took more books from the library rather than buying them; and started dipping into my savings and comingling inherited assets, two absolute no-nos according to every financial pundit's books I started to read when I visited bookstores, my new main solo social outing.

As Oprah advised, it's up to you to solve your problems. Stop whining. I tried by writing a novel with Margaret we titled *Dumped*. We thought this revenge fantasy might become a best seller and maybe a movie. I envisioned Anne Archer playing me—and being terrified when a process server jumped out in the middle of the night from a bush to serve papers. (It happened in real life, as did a PI following me to serve a subpoena.) Margaret picked Annette Bening as the perennial perky, cheer-you-on-always friend.

Here's the scenario: An octogenarian mother—probably Angela Lansbury (think *Murder, She Wrote* with a twist—does away with her son-in-law (pick all possible reasons you want), and ends up in a "coun-

try club–style" prison since she had no prior arrests or even driving
infractions. And while incarcerated, Mom finds joy in teaching inmates
to read and write akin to the late Jean S. Harris, helps improve the
prison's terrible, too carb-ish food with her nutrition background, and
gets to exercise daily in the prison's landscaped courtyard because of
her many good deeds. Best of all, she's released early after the judge is
besieged by other dumped females worldwide who saw the publicity
about what Mom did for jilted womankind.

We had such fun we wrote another novel, more light hearted, about
my running my dream job of a baking business, *Master Chef*, with my
eponymous business named Patty's Cakes. In the book, my sweet success made me deliriously happy, as well as a wealthy celebrity chef on
TV, magazine covers, invitations here and there—though it also made
my former husband, by now another burned-out attorney, so envious,
he resigned and started his own company, Sweet Tarts, and he wasn't
talking about me. Soon we went crust to crust for top celeb chef on the
Food Network TV station, and he tried to outdo me with a line of pots
and pans known as "Chez Sam," the moniker we had given him.

Just putting it all down on paper offered enough vindication since we
decided not to publish either and anger anybody—or put the kibosh on
my future dating prospects, who might fear for their lives (or at least
their waistlines).

Fantasy quickly shifted back to reality. I hunted desperately for
more work. The publishing world was changing rapidly as newspapers
were sold and magazines folded. Once my younger daughter was in
college, I reluctantly took a job in Chicago where I stayed at a friend's
home gratis during the week and commuted 10 hours round trip each
weekend to have regular income and build up a 401(k). At the same
time, I continued juggling the mechanics of a divorce and, trying to
maintain my ongoing freelance business, working early in the morning
and late at night.

After less than a year, I resigned because of exhaustion and applied
for temporary legal funds by filing a motion seeking relief *pendente lite*
(pen-den-tay lee-tay), Latin for "awaiting litigation." Most states, it
seems, have laws allowing the spouse without access to money the right
to come to court for this sort of temporary relief. The judge concurred
that I needed more monthly money, and that we should split the cost of
the mortgage until the house was sold, which the court ordered, and

also split the cost of the girls' college tuitions. That decision seemed unfair to me since I earned far less, but I learned all isn't fair.

Each month I worried if there would be enough money. Soon the bank began sending pre-foreclosure notices to the home address when the full mortgage amount wasn't received. My lawyer advised me not to cover all since I probably would never recoup the funds. My credit rating began to drop faster than the Dow on a bad day. And then the domino effect set in. When I went to visit both daughters at their respective colleges, the car rental company wouldn't accept my debit card or cash. I didn't have a credit card in good standing. I took a bus from one school to the other, which almost doubled the time. A friend picked me up at the bus stop, and I stayed at her home. Once home, I began begging my attorney more frequently in e-mails and hysterical, tearful calls to find a way to settle. He said doing so was impossible since no settlement offered by my husband's attorney could support me adequately and several didn't warrant a response.

I found myself sinking faster into financial quicksand. I comingled more inherited assets to bail myself out, not knowing that I wouldn't get those back, either. I asked my home insurance carrier to reimburse me for small problems including some basement leaks. The company did, but then abruptly cancelled my insurance after a pipe burst in the ravine on our property and flooded the basement, which it said was my third and final claim. Because there had been so many water claims throughout the city during a particularly wet spring and summer, getting new insurance proved impossible until I went to an excess lines carrier that handles troubled cases. It agreed to insure my home, but at triple the cost. I grabbed it.

My gut still told me not to cave in to the other side's offers. I eliminated more expenses and tried these ways to protect myself better for the future:

- I bought long-term care insurance I had read about since I knew I couldn't expect my daughters to care for me if a problem arose, and the insurance would be cheaper when I was younger and healthier. It was an investment in my future as a single at less than $100 a month at that time. To pay for it, I eliminated a daily small skim latte fix that would save me about the same amount.

- I found a new financial advisor since the one we shared during marriage now had a conflict of interest due to our divorce.
- I went to a new therapist since the ones we had consulted during our marriage focused on salvaging it; now it was time to salvage me. The therapist helped to restore my self-esteem and urged me not to believe all the criticisms leveled at me at the end of my marriage. The therapist also helped by encouraging me to be patient with myself. "You're still emotionally connected given your thirty years together. Your tears, even frequent tears, are good because they show you're grieving. This is all part of a process." The explanation helped intellectually, but not yet emotionally.
- I started keeping detailed records of everything I spent, both for the divorce and to know what I needed monthly in order to cut back more. I asked both daughters also to track their necessary expenses. Every single receipt went into separate files—grocery store, hairdresser, therapist, gym, house repairs, attorney fees, college books, transportation, doctors, dentists, and so on. I arranged the files in bins on my bedroom floor. This became command central for what felt like war.
- I invested more in me—a website to boost my business, more exercise classes to get trimmer and healthier as my blood pressure remained high due to stress, hair coloring, better makeup and some new clothing to look and feel better and market myself for dating. When I showed up at one store and inquired about sexier clothing, a favorite saleswoman asked, "What's going on? Are you getting divorced?" She had been through this drill many times. And I thought I was so original!
- I even contacted a psychic in Los Angeles I read about in a magazine, who advised me after reading my various numbers of my birthday and year, "Don't panic. . . . In a short time all this will be over and you will start a wonderful journey of prosperity. Life is cyclical and, as you know, chaos is part of our existence. Have faith and remember your journey, love of your family and incredible gift of expression." Margaret was skeptical and said, "It sounds like a Hallmark card. You can pay me. I could have told you all that. Don't you realize how vague she is?" I did but it made me feel better to believe that what lay ahead might be joyful.

- I asked my attorney if I could take on some of the legal legwork to cut expenses and because I knew as a diligent reporter I could piece together information. When it was time also to depose anyone on the other side, I insisted on attending as part of the legal team.

The divorce trial was one of the worst, emotionally gut-wrenching experiences of my life. The night before. I couldn't sleep or stop crying, and I worried how I'd cope in the future. My therapist called late to say don't buckle under at this point. By morning I was calmer, temporarily, and more worried about what I'd wear to convey the right look of a scorned wife: sensible black pantsuit for day #1, blue wool dress with discreet jewelry for a bit of color for day #2, and repeat of black pantsuit for the wrap-up since I wasn't spending lavishly on me. But I knew it didn't really matter.

Then for three very long days, we sat at tables within arm's length of one another in the city's drab courtroom. I watched my husband come in daily wearing one of the many natty ties I had purchased through the years. His attorneys arrived wheeling in oversized black briefcases bulging with papers. They—and sometimes witnesses—whispered to one another. I remembered some testimony was inaccurate and had no relevance except to embarrass me, or was said to justify a simple fact—divorcing spouses want out of the marriage and most with as short or no encumbered financial cord. His side brought in a career expert who was asked: Could she be retrained? How are her typing skills? Could she get a higher-paying position? I had worked for almost thirty years as a low-earning journalist, which had always seemed fine before for us, but now at more than fifty I was expected to land a more lucrative position. I would have loved to. I was embarrassed that strangers—the stenographer and bailiff—were hearing highly personal information, but I knew both had probably heard slightly different storylines through the years, another break-up, more heartache, more money tossed aside. I became numb, discouraged, yet somehow found inner strength to keep going as we waited for the judge's decree.

Months later the news came as I was driving. I nervously listened as my attorney's paralegal called and said the decision was in and to come to the office as soon as possible. I begged her to put one of my two attorneys on the phone to give me a short synopsis of what was decided.

We were pleased in many ways, disappointed in others, and I was told that judges often try to balance results to avoid an appeal. At the same time, my attorneys warned me they expected the other side to appeal.

In the meantime, with numbers in hand, I switched to another financial advisor who specialized in counseling divorced and widowed women and was recommended by a friend, also dumped. This advisor didn't make money on trades as my prior one had, but collected a percentage of assets invested with her. At the first meeting, she presented a power point of my assets and probable future. I sat there crying and left her office depressed, yet determined more than ever that somehow I would survive. We agreed:

- I had to sell the house before the market turned down, which a smart real-estate saleswoman predicted. "You don't need this house any longer; your girls aren't coming home," the salesperson told me bluntly. I listened and accepted the reality by looking for a rental until I knew where I would go permanently.
- My financial advisor suggested that I use only my debit card to avoid incurring credit card charges.
- She helped me develop a realistic budget to rebuild my credit rating and still enjoy life, but on a shoestring. I never liked valet parking but now I never used it, even if it meant only saving $3 or $4 each time. Walking was good for me. I learned how to make good coffee at home in lieu of my former Starbucks habit. I started using my Frequent Flyer miles, or would drive to visit friends in different cities and stay with them, rationalizing that it was more personal, and, of course, less expensive.
- I maintained some important rituals—hosting Thanksgiving, important to my daughters and included friends and family; and birthday celebrations, including for Margaret's sixtieth with a newly concocted "Megarita" drink named for her.

After the full seven years required to remove my bad credit rating, my scores rebounded, and my bank's loan officer told me I again represented a good mortgage risk. We celebrated with my home-baked cookies. Hardest was telling my daughters my financial situation had changed dramatically, and there were many things I no longer could afford to do with and for them. They seemed fine. My older daughter explained, "That's not why we love you."

With my house sold, my girls thriving—one in a job and the other in graduate school—and my funds invested wisely, I knew I had a tiny sum to burn for occasional luxuries: my version meant that full tank of gasoline; a pedicure sometimes in the dead of winter; entertaining guests, but not as part of a former duo expert in Julia Child's repertoire; and indulging sporadically by buying *People* magazine at the grocery store when the headlines screamed out to me, "Lance Armstrong retires after winning a record seventh consecutive Tour de France victory" in 2005.

Best of all, as my anger dissipated, I finally stopped telling my divorce story to anyone who asked. I was able to forgive, though not forget. I still worried about my financial future at the end of each month but a tiny bit less, and I believed my happiness quotient no longer was linked to lost dollars that we had worked so hard to save, or even anything related to someone who wanted nothing more to do with me. Now, it was about being the sole captain of my ship—even if only a rowboat. I started to navigate the new course ahead, determined to master lessons from all mistakes made.

Accepting Reality

There is no magic formula or preset timetable for handling a divorce or dealing with the death of a spouse. Some divorces are protracted and contentious—often when the stakes are high, though high is relative. Others are quick and amicable—often if fewer assets exist, children are involved, or both parties want to split and remain on "friendly" terms. And once a divorce is over or a death occurs, people move at different speeds to build a new future and try different ways to heal. Margaret, who never expected to lose a spouse because she was in total denial that her husband's cancer could end his life, continued to work and went to therapy. It took two years for her to begin to feel joy again. Barbara's divorce was long and drawn out. The end of the marriage seemed to her to come out of the blue. Cracks in the relationship had emerged, but she thought they were due to nonmarital reasons. She believed most long-term marriages face different challenges at one time or another that require work on each side's part. Once she accepted there was no hope, however, she focused on her daughters, mother, work, pursuing old passions such as painting. Slowly, she rebuilt her life. She also was eager, some thought frantic, to meet someone new since she wasn't yet comfortable with being alone.

For others, such as Jayne C., lessons came slower. Both of her marriages ended in acrimonious divorces. Husband No. 1 was verbally abusive and condescending. After three years of dating she married husband No. 2, and he moved into her home, but he wasn't the successful business person he claimed to be. He had been dishonest about his finances, was paying alimony to his ex-wife, and the couple was stretched financially due to house improvements. Whenever he could, he spent days and weekends away attending car races. Their intimacy subsided, they talked less, and did almost nothing together. One Sunday after being away racing cars all weekend, he came home and simply said, "I'm out of here." The next day he came by, took all his belongings and filed for divorce leaving Jayne in worse shape financially than before and requiring her to sell her house and start life all over again. Unfortunately for her, he had no financial responsibility to her due to the shortness of their marriage—only six years.

It took two failed marriages for Jayne to learn the importance of living on her own and loving herself. Jayne had always been proud of her figure, but during her unhappy second marriage she had gained pounds and started to let herself go. After her husband left, she took charge and started to work out weekly with a trainer and eat better on her own. She was rightfully proud when a friend had to loan her jeans since nothing she owned fit.

Divorced from husband No. 1, Nancy H. met and married husband No. 2 seven years later. However, they divorced after four years because of differences about the importance of family and how to spend their hard-earned dollars. After seeing two therapists and going back and forth about whether to split, the coup de grace came when Nancy realized she couldn't be married to someone who wanted to live beyond his means. Nancy had a prenup, which at the time was fine with her soon-to-be husband. He told her that, in the unlikely case they should divorce, he would not pay alimony. Both knew the stakes if they split. And when they did, their divorce was amicable, expeditious, and clear-cut, albeit sad and gut-wrenching. The only asset to divide was their home. He bought out her half after having the home valued. Unfortunately, Nancy lost money from her initial contribution for the down payment because its value went south after the recession. The only time Nancy and her ex talked after the divorce was to meet at a Starbucks to sign papers to file their taxes jointly. Nancy hopes to meet someone new. She greatly misses the companionship, but for now she says she never cares to marry again.

3

MISSING MARRIED LIFE

MARGARET

INCHING FORWARD

We were at the stage of life of so many possibilities—retirement, financial security, kids grown and gainfully employed; time to travel and explore, volunteer, and spend our hard-earned money on ourselves. And then in almost a flash, it was over; my future derailed. In the throes of overwhelming grief, what I really wanted to do was to drink beyond my normal single glass or two of wine. What I did was healthier. As a way to remember him intimately, I made a list of all the things that I missed most after living with my husband for 42 years—even his quirks that could be so annoying, such as never loading the dishwasher or eating leftovers. But through it all, he was the love of my life.

- The "Jewish mother" in our relationship who hovered and worried excessively: telling our oldest child to wear a jacket, our youngest not to forget his passport when traveling abroad, and our grown daughter to wear socks and call when she arrived any place, no matter what time.
- A father who never left one of our kids standing in front of a school in a storm waiting to be picked up because he was chronically early; who drove with our daughter across the country when

she moved, and then helped get her settled; or who schlepped mattresses and furniture up six flights of stairs when our youngest moved east.

- The frugal one who kept me in check, although I am far from a spendthrift. For example, he loved to stay in cheap motels with plastic-wrapped glasses, skinny bars of soap, generic shampoos and conditioners, and rooms with coat racks rather than full closets. Once we retired, we hoped to stay in more upscale hotels.

- A dance partner at weddings, Bar Mitzvahs, and black-tie galas. He loved to dance and had fabulous rhythm, all dating from his earliest days as a drummer.

- A roaring temper that reared its ugly head when he felt crossed, one of the kids did something unacceptable, or he couldn't get an agent on a helpline. But, he often ended up laughing at himself for being so serious at times and initially lacking that sense of humor.

- Squabbler, complainer, misunderstanding master. I liked to fight and taught him how to do so fairly. What a mistake! He became an expert and improved on my skill.

- Raising our three children together and taking great joy in their accomplishments, as only parents will do, even if their accomplishments weren't so great. But loving that they each pursued something in the arts—music or theater in some way, passions of his.

- Someone in the house to help me. He'd carry and lift things; move furniture, TV sets, window AC units, and other heavy objects. He did it even if it gave him a hernia (it did), and he did it graciously.

- Someone to laugh with—he could be hysterically funny—who had the same values politically and liked the same movies and books, most of the time, as I. Oh, there was the night I made him watch *Pride and Prejudice* at a movie theater, and he brought a pillow to sleep through it.

- Lover of low-priced eateries and cafeterias that reminded me of dining in a senior center, though the advantage to him were the great prices and knowledge that we often were the youngest.

- Someone to celebrate with who knew what I loved and made a big deal out of birthdays and anniversaries. He'd buy flowers, bring me candy, include the kids at a fancy restaurant, and skip using his usual clipped coupons.

- The crinkling of cellophane in a totally silent concert hall; he always had to have his hard candy and red and black licorice.
- Someone with whom to take yoga and laugh so hard we got kicked out of the class, go to computer classes with, help flood victims with their ruined homes and furnishings, peruse museums, take Sunday drives, walk in the park with our dog, share a glass of fabulous wine he had just discovered.
- Not having every single event video recorded—from our children's concerts, to parties and every friend's kid's concert and party. At each event, I would hold my hands over my face and shout, "Don't take me. Enough. I look terrible."
- Someone who stood up for me always and stood his ground for what he believed about every situation—even issues in my family's business—and being magnanimous when things didn't go his way.
- Someone who accepted and loved my family, all of them, even when it proved difficult at times.
- Listening to him crunch potato chips and popcorn and twist off the top of a soda can in bed each night while we watched Turner Classic Movies.
- Getting out his sports car on a beautiful spring or summer day, taking down the top, grabbing me and our dog for a ride, and spending time talking.
- Just being each other's good friend and knowing that I was adored most of the time.
- Bringing home new T-shirts from liquor manufacturers and wineries and our often wearing matching shirts that said such things as: *Blue Nun: Revive the Habit.*
- Standing his ground about not eating at restaurants that didn't purchase his wine lines, even when friends wanted to go to a certain place.
- The one person who knew me better than I knew myself and vice versa because we were part of each other's lives for so long, though it wasn't nearly long enough.

Others Move Forward

I could never imagine dating, let alone remarrying, but I began to hear and witness some happy stories, initially in the grief support group I had joined. Some of the best focused on what the group members missed about being married. One came from Joan, who had met her late husband Mike when they were fifteen years old. They dated for eight years, although they attended different colleges. "I was so in love with Mike that I wanted to quit school and get married. He urged me to get my degree as a special education teacher, and in retrospect, I am so glad he did," says Joan, who still works full-time for her city's special school district. On June 17, 1978, they wed.

Joan's thirty-two-year marriage to Mike was good and solid but definitely had its ups and downs. Joan says, "As we got older, our love grew more, and I depended so much on him. We have two great kids. There were some hard times, too, like when Mike lost his job in his fifties as a mechanical engineer. Most of our fights were about money. I wanted to spend more than he did, although we planned well financially. I handled the daily bills, and Mike managed our financial portfolio. But when he tried to show me what was where, I was disinterested."

Throughout their marriage, Mike had been a healthy, hearty man. Then one day Mike had so much trouble breathing, "he couldn't walk from the chair to the bathroom," says Joan. He was rushed to the hospital where they discovered an explosive form of lung cancer. While there with his health deteriorating, Mike discussed finances and investments with Joan and their son. They had a will and talked about what he wanted at his funeral. Five weeks after being admitted to the hospital, Mike died. He was fifty-five.

Joan found a grief counselor to help her through the initial months of pain of losing someone so quickly. One year later, she joined our grief support group that would turn her life around. It was there that she met Mike 2.0. While spilling her guts to the group about the loss of her husband, No. 2 Mike was sitting across the table grieving for the loss of his wife of more than thirty years. "After several months, Mike began to notice that the details of his marriage mirrored those of mine. He began to feel a connection and wanted to get to know me better outside the group," says Joan.

Their relationship started clandestinely with e-mails back and forth, until Mike asked Joan to dinner. It was March 3, 2012, and her late husband had been gone one-and-a-half years. "I was very nervous about it, but went. It was strange also that I would be going out with another man named Mike." On their first date at Olive Garden, Joan took out a scrapbook about her late husband to show the new Mike. "He handled it so well," she says. They had a great time that evening and Joan thought, "I could talk some more with this man. I didn't want to leave."

On the second date, they walked in a park while Joan read three pages of notes she wrote about why she wasn't getting into a relationship. "My heart belonged to Mike No. 1. If Mike No. 2 wanted more, he could go elsewhere. He seemed okay with this. And each time we went out, I said to myself: 'No, no I'm not going to get serious' and then it kept developing into more."

Joan remembers holding hands with Mike No. 2 for the first time. "We were sitting on my sofa and he asked, 'May I put my arm around you?' He did. I started crying. Neither of us had ever been intimate with anyone other than our late spouses." It was four months into their relationship when they decided to sleep together. "We went to my house, got into my bed, and I started sobbing. I wasn't ready." A couple weeks later, I told him I thought I was prepared to try again. We took a weekend and rented a cabin. I was so nervous, I brought Xanax. Mike asked for one, too." On March 3, 2015, three years after their first date, Joan and Mike No. 2 became engaged.

Today, Joan says she has a good life and her advice about dating, especially after a long happy marriage, resonated with me though I was far from ready to follow her example. Yet, I tucked away her advice just in case: "Realize your heart can open again; it's really big enough. It's also healthy to find someone who is different from your late spouse. Mike No. 1 was very physical, well balanced, sanguine, and adventurous, but he didn't talk a lot about his feelings. Mike No. 2 is more intense and touchy-feely. We can talk candidly about loneliness, sadness, love, and anger. Fortunately, our values are similar. Most important, I'm so grateful that I allowed myself to date Mike No. 2, as much as I fought it. Loving again unleashes another side of you."

BARBARA

UNRAVELING

I was terrified when I knew I couldn't save my marriage; one person never can. It takes teamwork, togetherness, giving in to the other more than you think you should at times, yet never counting. I wasn't going to give up easily, however. I have always been tenacious in my relation-ships and work. I agreed to the counseling he asked for, which in retrospect may have been his way to air out loud his unhappiness about all the transgressions he felt I had caused through the years. At our first session with a woman neither of us knew, so she would come with an open mind, he ticked off all the horrible ways he said I had acted from a long list on a yellow legal pad. I sat sipping coffee with tears streaming down my face, which I tried to hide by putting on my sunglasses as the deeds stretched on and on. We walked out of the office together, stood at the elevator in silence, went down to the parking lot and our separate cars, and I remember saying despite my deep hurt and shock, some-thing to the effect, "See you at home later for dinner."

I twisted myself into a pretzel to try to change his mind. I got skinny, wore more youthful sexier clothing, served nice hors d'oeuvres and wine when he got home from work to whet his appetite for me, prom-ised the moon, sun, and stars—and beyond—and swore I wouldn't be the one to file for divorce or first hire a lawyer. I hoped that delaying the decision would change his mind. We tried another therapist when he was unhappy with the first, this time his choice. It was in her office that he told me he no longer loved me. I felt I had been punched in the gut for this to be announced the first time with a stranger listening to my words and watching my body movements.

Even after he moved out, I kept trying and was delighted when seemingly out of the blue, he suggested trying again. We went to a third therapist, one I had been seeing, who urged us to date. But it was too late. The "us" had slowly vanished. I accepted he had no interest in working on the marriage. It was time for me to begin to make decisions totally on my own that were best for me and, in many cases, for our daughters. I certainly didn't miss the acrimony or feeling of deep alone-ness. But I was resolute not to let our breakup embitter me forever about him or our thirty-one-year union. I still don't believe that he never was happy; neither do most friends and family members. What I do know is that we simply didn't win the ultimate prize—"till death do us part." Here's what I missed most:

- A history where you can mention someone's name, place, or important milestone from twenty or thirty years ago and not provide an explanation; the quenelles at that charming restaurant and inn in the south of France, so delicious we hurried back to eat them again, or that proud feeling when he gave a clever, funny toast at our older daughter's Bat Mitzvah.
- Someone who knew your family and oldest friends, as you knew theirs, and accepted them, at least most of the time, even when it was tortuous.
- The continuity of planning toward a shared future, especially when big hurdles seemed to be whether to retire some day by mountains he loved or water you craved, rather than divide up the photos by a divorce decree.
- Knowing someone so well that you share inside jokes about people and places and know what they think, will say, do, read, watch, order, and are willing to give them a "put and call" if they like what you chose better than theirs—whether food, an airplane seat, or section of a newspaper.
- Having someone who calls you daily to check in at the same time—then sometimes multiple times a day when you least expect it, and lets you know when they're coming home at night.
- Someone who's also by your side whether waiting in any line, car seat, family photo, or in bed.
- The first one to clink your glass and say "Happy New Year," or *l'chaim.*
- Someone who knows your deepest fears and doesn't make fun of them, no matter how trivial or even nonsensical, including rituals such as when flying and making a contribution to a certain charity for good luck, wearing a certain good luck bracelet, or talking to the pilot to find out if the flight plan would be turbulent.
- Someone you can rejoice with about your shared children's highs and sympathize about their lows; nobody else cares as much as you do together.

- Someone with whom to think through big decisions—from buying a house, fixing up a kitchen, or taking on big, new assignments for work.
- Someone you want to help reach a goal, then another, and another, and whose accomplishments and disappointments mean more to you than your own.
- Someone who has cute nicknames for you, which are slightly embarrassing so you rarely share them with others.
- Someone whose opinion you keep respecting, whom you still like and, yes, still love, and want to be with forever.
- Someone with whom you remember when you had to scrimp and save and could only eat two meals a day on vacation but promised when you had more money you'd go back and eat a third—and even off the expensive à la carte menu.
- Someone whose moods you can read instantly—for example, a wrinkled brow—and vice versa, without explaining.
- Someone who knows when you're having a terrible day, tolerates your bad mood, lets you get angry, and accepts your apology before you apologize.
- Someone who can be brutally honest about things you've done when you're not your best when it's really important.
- Someone who has your back and always forgives you, and lets you forgive them. Otherwise, the ball game is over.

4

SELF-PRESERVATION

MARGARET

TREADING WATER

Everyone knew. I quickly went into hiding.

Then two months after my husband died, I decided it was time for me to do something I swore I'd never be able to do again: Open the door to human contact. Of course, I didn't really mean I would never reemerge from my house. I had to at some point. But I still fantasized about moving to an alien planet where strange beings didn't know who I was, didn't care, and certainly didn't speak my language. They'd leave me alone since they might fear me and my deep grief.

Deep down I craved attention, pampering, and largesse of family and close friends to get me through and back to the land of the functioning. It was all the acquaintances and strangers I didn't want to have to chat with and explain my story, again, and again, as profound changes began to take place in my life.

If I had to pick the next low point, it was that first day I returned to work after my husband's death. I was a nervous wreck and made the neurotic Woody Allen in his movie *Take the Money and Run* look calm and act composed. Could I don a disguise, wear a wig, big sunglasses like Woody? What a silly idea. That would draw even more attention to me.

Once I went out in public again, and back to work, what would people say? How would they greet me? Would they avoid me or hover to make sure I was OK? Would they look at me in a sad, patronizing way? Include me at lunch? Check up on me by stopping into my office or e-mailing me constantly? Would my boss stop giving me work out of fear I couldn't handle assignments because I would cry nonstop? But what did I really want them to do? I was ambivalent. I eventually found my feelings changed and evolved as days and weeks went on.

The same was true for Robin W. who lost her husband of 26 years to a five-year illness. "At first I was in a fog, gliding along and not worrying about money or taking care of myself or much of anything. I was holed up in my house and in my bedroom most of the time. Some days I wouldn't eat and would just sit in front of the TV and stare at the screen. I really got into the *Twilight* series—so ridiculous, but it was a fabulous escape. I thought all would be okay, that some special spirit from the other side would come and take care of me. It finally hit me one day that I had to get off my ass and be strong for my sons. It was time to start moving forward in a different way."

In the meantime, my returning to work and everyone else's reaction, as well as mine, became a major topic of conversation at grief support sessions. Each of us was finding our way. Mary talked about going to her neighbor to get permission to ask her husband to help with small tasks around the house. Pat who had a friend tell her, "Get over it already, it's been long enough," told how she lost that friend when she said angrily, "I'm not ready. Don't tell me how to feel." And Rita M., whose friends avoided calling because she kept crying on the phone, eventually understood that they couldn't cope with her intense grief, so she stopped taking those calls. Before long they stopped calling. How dare supposed friends act as they did, we thought collectively. If only they really knew what we were going through, they'd become empathetic and know exactly what to say, to ask, to do—and also what NOT to say and do.

Robin recalls that one of the questions she was asked most often was, "'Are you dating? Do you want to marry again?' I just wanted to run away and hide. Thinking about a new relationship was as far from my mind as possible." And she continued to avoid most people for more than a year until she started a part-time job that a friend had suggested to her. She recalls, "The routine, contact with people on a daily basis and the money—albeit not terrific"—gave her a feeling of being able to spend money freely on herself, which at the time was a lifesaver.

I now grasp not knowing all the proper sensitive etiquette when tragedy steps in. In the past, I, too, often was unsure, afraid to intrude on a person's grief, or ask the open-ended, unhelpful question: "How may I help?" Before my loss, I never could have fathomed what it was like. As the Cherokee tribe of Native Americans would say, "Don't judge a man until you have walked a mile in his moccasins." But when I was in those shoes for the first time, I discovered they hurt in so many places. That would take time getting used to, if ever.

I know that feelings can be conflicting and take time to resolve; mine did. It has all been part of the grieving—and learning—process.

What I Wish People Had Said When Nolan Was Ill

1. What may I do for you? How about coffee tomorrow, if you have time in the afternoon? I have some great gossip to share and make you laugh.
2. I'm going to treat you to a massage; give me times and dates when you're available.
3. I'm getting a pedicure tomorrow and will pick you up so we can go together, if that works.
4. I'm going to the grocery store and bookstore: What would you like at both? I'll drop anything off and not even come in.
5. Have I told you enough what a terrific guy Nolan is; I'm rooting for both him and you.

What I Wish People Hadn't Asked When Nolan Was Ill

1. How did he get sick?
2. What's wrong with him?
3. Did you contact other hospitals and in other cites?
4. Did you get a second opinion, and where?
5. Is it serious and will he get better?
6. I know what you're going through and how you feel. (No you don't.)
7. How can you work full-time?

8. He doesn't look sick; how sick could he be?

What I Wish People Hadn't Asked or Said When He Died

1. How long was he ill and was it painful?
2. What exactly caused his death?
3. Are you OK financially?
4. Will you stay in your house or move, and where?
5. Do you think you'll date—and if so, when? When do you think you'll marry again?
6. Do you want to be fixed up? We can double when you're dating.
7. He's in a better place; at least he's no longer suffering.

What I Wish People Would Have Said Afterward—And Some Did

1. Do you need help around the house? I like to organize stuff and can be there tomorrow or the next day.
2. Would you just like to be left alone? If so, let me know your favorite thing to read or to eat and I'll drop it at your door.
3. I'm sure you hate walking into an empty house; let me meet you the first couple weeks at the front door and make sure you're safe.
4. May I walk your dog for you if you don't feel OK to leave the house? I'll feed him, too.
5. How are your parents doing? I'm going to send a card or give them a call to make sure they're OK; I'd also like to write Nolan's mom even though she didn't know me well.

What People Did That Most Pleased and Consoled Me

1. A group of friends and neighbors hosted the shiva after the funeral, organizing all the food purchases, setting all out, cleaning all up, and putting leftovers in the fridge.
2. One couple did a home wine tasting in my late husband's honor with my kids and their friends pouring great wines from their cellar.

3. One couple invited all of us for Passover.
4. One friend sent flowers on the first anniversary Nolan and I missed sharing, and she also gave me a pedicure to a favorite special spa.
5. One friend started helping me clean out my house and organizing all to take to sell.
6. One of my sisters, who helped me write thank you notes, accompanied me to buy the gravestone after I wrote more than 25 different epitaphs and sent them around to family and friends to pick the one they liked best.
7. Many of my family and closest friends call each year on our anniversary, his birthday, and the day of his death
8. Many couples included me so I wouldn't be alone on major holidays and New Year's Eve.
9. A childhood friend made my favorite cookies and dropped them off at my door.
10. Many of my girlfriends with handy husbands or partners and family pitched in and fixed things in the house and when I moved to my condo, hanged some of my paintings.
11. A partner of a good friend came and sat in my apartment the day I moved to meet the movers and told them where to put everything and how to arrange the furniture.
12. Many keep sharing stories about Nolan—all his strengths and his wonderful quirks; they help me keep his memory alive.

I am now a member of one of the most unwanted clubs in the world. Although I wish I could resign or be voted out, I learned how to be a better, caring friend to others during and after a crisis. Gradually, I adjusted—and most, I hope, will, too. Robin has met someone who she's been dating for two years with no plans to marry in the near future. "I'm just having a good time," she reports.

BARBARA

SEEKING A WITNESS PROTECTION PROGRAM FOR DUMPED WOMEN

I was not prepared for the aftermath of the breakup of my marriage and how public it would become.

The night after we returned from dropping our older daughter at college, my husband told me he planned to divorce me and would be moving into a rental apartment. I quickly called my mother and a handful of my closest friends, who had become my circle of confidantes as my marriage fell apart in its last year. I was very selective about whom I trusted. I lived in a big city but a small suburb, and all of a sudden my surroundings became claustrophobic. It happens in any community, but news—especially juicy gossip—always seemed to travel as fast and furiously as a contagion. I wanted to shield myself from the embarrassment I felt about being dumped and tossed aside. I also didn't want to draw attention to myself or my children.

Yet, despite my circumspection, word leaked out. It always does. The morning after I learned I would be divorced, Margaret called and said, "So-and-so just called and said she heard that you are separated. She wants to know if it's true. I told her nothing, of course. I said, 'What are you talking about?'" I immediately panicked and called the gossip columnist at the newspaper where I had worked. He had his pulse on everything in our community, and I knew he wouldn't put anything in the paper or share information if I asked him not to. He kept his promise and seemed concerned about how I was doing. Next I worked the phone lines to share the news with others who should know or would hear, including our rabbi and some of my spouse's relatives with whom I had developed tight bonds. And then, I tried to go into hiding. If there had been a witness protection program for dumped women to begin a new life, I would have signed up.

Once I was alone in my house, I developed a survival strategy:

- Fearing I would run into anyone I knew, I stopped going to the grocery store near my home and went to one farther away.

- I stopped going to the gym, except with one close friend who had met me at the tail end of my marriage and became very protective. She and her husband were the first ones to invite me out to dinner as a solo; I began inviting them over to reciprocate, and they always asked every weekend what I was doing, told me their plans, and never let me be alone both nights unless they were out of town.
- I frequently visited a close friend's house late at night. She had insomnia and many nights when I was upset, I drove the few miles to her home, headed into a cheerful garden room where I could stretch out on a floral patterned sofa, and talk nonstop, as if I were in a shrink's office.
- I went for frequent long walks with another older friend who had known me since I had moved to the Midwest. She was sweet and compassionate, listened well, kept my confidences, and never pried. Her husband also joined in some of our conversations, and I desperately needed a male point of view.
- I took my daughters to Los Angeles, invited by close friends to stay in their home for a week of just hanging out.

Eventually, I took the counsel of a friend in another city who said, "You have nothing to be embarrassed about. Hold your head high, smile when you run into people you know and continue to live your life." I tried with baby steps. And I also listened to Margaret's wise words that I would soon be an old story that nobody would care about. "You're only in the headlines until there's something newer and juicer for many to talk about." She was right most of the time, though I found that some became "tragedy whores" as Carole Radziwill dubbed them in her book, *What Remains: A Memoir of Fate, Friendship and Love*, when she lost her husband Anthony, John F. Kennedy Jr.'s cousin. Many of these folks thrived on bad news and made a beeline to my door. I also learned to be prepared when asked how I was doing. As a matter of course, I smiled and cheerily said by rote, "OK!" whether I was or wasn't.

Surprisingly, there were milestones that I relished. My older daughter was sharing her transition to college life, which required a certain amount of adjustment for each of us. For her, it meant going from a small high school in the Midwest to a large university in the East, located almost in the middle of a scenic nowhere. She needed me to listen to the ups and downs, as well as hear about her classes, luck in drawing a good roommate, making new friends—many from my home state of New York, dating, eagerness to join a sorority, and games played by her college's highly respected ice hockey team, for which I had prepared her with a copy of *Ice Hockey for Dummies*.

My younger daughter and I developed new routines and a special closeness we hadn't shared when two others were present. Now it was just the two of us. I had always cooked from scratch for my family, but I became paralyzed and started bringing in take-out. She rebelled, "We need to cook for us." We did, and Margaret helped by bringing over her homemade chili, chocolate chip cookies, and tart lemon bars. Then my youngest daughter and I also started a tradition. We had always dined as a family of four without the TV on. She suggested we had become so bonded and talked so much that we could instead watch together her favorite shows. With plates balanced on our laps in our family room, it was *Seventh Heaven* on Mondays, *Dawson's Creek* Tuesdays, *The Gilmore Girls* Wednesdays, and *Friends* Thursdays. I became hooked and intimately involved in the characters' lives. Friday and Saturday my daughter was with friends, always asking first if it was OK to leave me alone.

I didn't want her feeling sorry for me. In fact, I didn't want anyone to think I was a victim. But I started to compile a list of what I wish people had said and not said as I moved through the divorce process, learning that the wheels of justice move slowly but the gossip lines heat up quickly. Since then, I've learned that others feel the same way at times. I asked a work colleague turned friend, Rhonda S., who went through two divorces and continues to battle cancer, to share her responses to the barrage of questions and comments she—and most women who lose a spouse to death or divorce—endure:

How are you doing? "'Better than ever,' or 'great,' is what I'd say to people I barely knew. Maybe, I'm jaded but I felt so many wanted to know just for gossip. A lot didn't ask me since I had been married twice and briefly—five years the first time and four years the second. In both cases, people rarely got to know us as couples."

Will you start to date? "Few asked. I had bigger concerns. After the second divorce, I had a child who was three years old, so I usually responded, 'I'm going to raise my child and do what I have to do.' If people insisted on knowing more, I'd usually add, 'If someone interesting comes along who can enhance my life I will. I don't need a room-mate to come home to and talk about, "How was your day, honey?" And I certainly don't want to stay up past 7:30 p.m. after usually being exhausted.' After my first divorce, nobody asked since we had the shared tragedy of losing a child, which caused the breakup of the marriage."

Is your daughter OK? "I always said, 'She's fine,' or 'great and having a great life.' By the time she was old enough to realize she didn't have a father living with her as many friends did, it was harder. And, she often saw her father only on weekends for a few hours. But she had my Dad around as a father figure. I usually just didn't discuss it with others."

Do you have a good lawyer? "Nobody ever asked this because by the time they might have asked, I was finished with the divorce process, done, washed my hands of it."

Will you be financially OK? "My family asked that, but nobody I didn't know well or even a bit did, maybe because so many people knew I had been the breadwinner. I got more of the, 'How are you going to raise a child alone?' I always responded, smiling, 'We'll find out, won't we?' That stopped the conversation. And we were OK since when I traveled for a few days I took her with me. One time we went to a ranch in Kentucky, and I remember her walking with the owner to see an Arabian horse. My daughter was wearing her little red coat with a velvet collar. She sat at a table crayoning while I interviewed the rancher. He certainly didn't mind. Now, she's thirty years old, my partner in busi-ness, and tells me she learned her work ethic from me."

You know you were the one we were friendly with and cared about, right? "I think lots of people think they're comforting you when they say that—that if they talk badly, it will make you feel good, but it doesn't. It usually only reminds you that you were once part of a couple and happy. I would want to say to anybody who said that, 'Don't you know I wouldn't be in this situation having this conversation with you if all had been so great?' I have a big mouth, so it really depends on your person-ality and what you're comfortable saying."

I can have lunch any time: when's good? "I only said once, to a lunch rather than dinner invitation, what I really wanted to say, 'So, you didn't invite me because I'm not with someone?' The person responded, 'Yeah, I have to tell you, it's just three couples who have something in common.' I felt terrible and realized this is part of life. I was also often left out when couples I knew who had second homes went away together. I learned to go out with those female friends for lunch."

And for me, visiting my college-age daughter on my own the first time made me feel incredibly alone as I watched other parents in Noah's ark-style pairs share the visit with their children. I learned over time to recognize the pluses. We found we had great Mom-and-daughter-togetherness, and I felt a surge of independence being able to navigate travel on my own. By the time of my younger daughter's first parents' weekend, I had decided to invite my mother along as my partner. My daughter was the only one with a grandmother in tow.

I also found the truth in a childhood friend's counsel that I would meet many interesting single people and broad-minded couples in my new single status. I did, and most of all I learned the importance of being alone as my then-therapist advised. "You have to find you can do this," he said. He was right. I also learned by observing my mother who had been a widow for eight years and bravely started over at age 75, moving from her suburban home to New York City, joining a new temple, serving on the board of her neighborhood association, and participating in multiple book clubs. Change is rarely easy, but as Friedrich Nietzsche said: "That which does not kill us makes us stronger." I was still very much alive and felt empowered in my new role.

5

SHOW ME THE MONEY

MARGARET

SWEEPING REALITY AND MONEY UNDER THE MATTRESS

The only debt I had when my husband died was our mattress. It sounds ridiculous, but it was a fancy, thickly padded, German-made design that cost more than the down payment on many of our first cars.

The day we went mattress shopping was good. Just the two of us went from one store to another, throwing our bodies down on beds and rolling around to test them. We laughed hard and had a wonderful time, acting like two teenagers pretending we were playing house. It added some levity to what had become a very sad, difficult period, and brought to mind how much superficial tasks helped us deflect the seriousness of Nolan's illness. Rather than face his progressively worsening health, it was wonderful to focus on almost silly purchases: buying a mattress; two, giant, flat-screen TVs to entertain him while he spent hours in bed or lounging in the family room after a chemotherapy treatment; or heading to a wig store after he lost his thick head of hair, which so many peers had always envied. He still was able to make jokes as he tried on many wigs. "This looks like a dead animal on my head," he said laughing, reaching for another, and then another.

When I tried to bring up a serious, important discussion of our finances, he'd shut down or bark, "I don't want to discuss it now," or, "I'm too tired," or "Later." In his mind, I know he harbored that magical thinking that if he ignored dying, it wouldn't happen. So we both lived in denial and in the moment, a prime example of how easy it can be to fail to communicate simply by avoiding what matters.

Throughout our marriage, Nolan was the designated household financial person. He paid all bills, budgeted, figured out and paid taxes, invested our money. Everything. I gladly let him take on these tasks because I didn't like doing them and I didn't think I was good at math or being organized. I was the creative one. Once he was gone, I was totally unprepared for what I'd face trying to get my financial house in order.

This became a full-time job as I had to play a Colombo-style detective trying to piece together what assets we had; where important documents were kept, including the CDs he had purchased and how much my late husband had paid for them initially; and other investments. I also went searching for his 401(k), and in whose name everything was held. We had no master list. I didn't even have a clue what I had to live on, and, of course, no longer had his income. I felt I was too young to take Social Security. He had life insurance, but I didn't know how much. I had my salary, which was minimal, so I worried if it would suffice. Fortunately, I still had my job for a nonprofit, my 403(b), and a pension.

I was mortified when I found how little I knew and impulsively cancelled all magazine and newspaper subscriptions, even though I was a journalist and voracious reader. I also cut the cable stations; dropped a club membership; piled on sweaters and socks and lowered the heat; used as little hot water as possible and learned to jump in and out when I'd take a shower; waited until the dishwasher and washing machine were absolutely filled to run them; and began to check prices obsessively at the grocery store, Target, and Old Navy, where I mostly shopped. I became a relentless coupon clipper.

Our attorney suggested that I start with our CPA and tax forms to find the paper trail of what we owned and where it was located, and then go through Nolan's checkbook, past credit card statements, and even his wallet to discover recurring bills and expenses. Before I could do anything, I had to transfer accounts in both names into mine—

insurance, cell phone, credit cards, frequent flyer miles, city govern-
ment taxes for property, and personal taxes. It was an enormous challenge.

I remember calling Charter, the cable service, to cancel HBO and
got a customer service rep who said she could talk only to Nolan Crane
because his name was on the account. "But he passed away, and I don't
think he'll be calling you," I explained. I got nowhere. But I would show
them. I called back, got a different person, and said I was Nolan Crane.
"That's a strange name for a woman," she said. "Yes, my parents wanted
a boy," I replied.

I also had to show proof that he had died. I wasn't going to schlep
everyone to the cemetery, but I had the death certificate, which I had
to produce repeatedly at three investment companies, six banks (since
he had spread out our funds), and his life insurance company. One of
my sisters stayed with me after the funeral to drive me to all these
places. The rest I handled by mail. It took almost two months to complete the task, but I did it and was enormously proud of myself. Then, I
had to decide what to do with our assets.

I needed a trusted financial advisor. I asked everyone I knew for
suggestions. I was advised in every case to choose someone who
charged a percentage of my assets, and ask in advance how much that
would be, rather than someone who received a commission for every
trade, which could be a potential conflict of interest, an incentive for
the person to constantly buy and sell. I was told to ask for a written plan,
and if it would cost me. I narrowed it down to four—three women and
one man, all of whom I interviewed individually. I called my brother-in-
law, a New York lawyer, who helped me develop pointed questions. I
was good at asking tough questions for articles and thought, hey, I'm
interviewing these people. I also discovered that some people may decide to go with more than one financial person. I decided to stick with
one who would oversee the healthfulness of my finances like a primary
care physician and only call in a specialist if needed.

The woman I chose was willing to hold my hand and quarterback a
team of people to help me with anything that touched on my financial
affairs. She advised me to go through every check my husband had
written the year before and tally how much we spent on every aspect of
our lives on a monthly basis: home, utilities, tuitions, books, magazines,
classes, club, entertainment, wine, water, sewer, lawn, pool, movies,

restaurants. The list went on and on. We then designed an income plan and investment portfolio to generate enough income to last the length of my life, if nothing changed. We developed a "what-if" list if things did change. Maybe I'd win the lottery, write a best seller, make a killing on the sale of my house. We also discussed what my goal was. I decided it was to live adequately but frugally off interest and dividends, if possible, and leave most of the principal for my children's inheritance.

After six months, I felt relieved. I knew I wouldn't live in the lap of luxury—stay home and eat bonbons in bed while watching movies. Those never were my life's dreams. I knew that I would be OK, could breathe easier, go out again, buy books and my favorite candy, and even order a daily subscription to the *New York Times* again, one of my biggest indulgences.

Though I've learned in life not to focus on "shoulds," I know now what I should have done financially before Nolan got sick. Fortuitously, we had saved and invested our money. However, without these resources, the situation would have been much grimmer. This general information and knowledge I gleaned from going through a financial quagmire can aid others to plan better regardless of your financial situation:

1. Become financially savvy. If you don't understand and read your monthly financial statements or daily stock prices because they can make you cross-eyed (I used to get the envelopes and shove them in a drawer), learn to do so. Ignoring your financial status is like ignoring your health—dangerous! You can take a course at a community college, buy some basic book primers, go online, or ask your financial advisor to explain essentials. Nobody will pay as much attention to numbers and directions of investments as you will. Then, do so; it's like brushing and flossing your teeth daily. But don't get neurotic about market blips; you need to learn to understand market cycles and be in the market for the long haul, however long that is.
2. Get a lawyer and write and update your wills, if you haven't done so. Be sure that your spouse has given you a durable power of attorney for finances. This is a document that allows you to make decisions if your spouse is incapacitated. Your spouse should also have one from you. Even if you're both in great health, it's never

too early to plan. Something catastrophic may occur. If you do this together, at least you know what you have and where it's kept—at least half the battle, probably more. Have information available both on paper and digitally. Make sure all your financial providers have a copy of the Powers of Attorney, and have them confirm to you by paper or e-mail that they will honor your POA. Some firms may require their own forms.

3. Get a living will and health directive. Sometimes this document is also called a power of attorney for health care. Whatever it's called in your state, this document stipulates what to do in case of a medical crisis—do or do not intubate, do or do not use a feeding tube, do or do not resuscitate. Again, have this available on paper and digitally. Make sure the person who will make your health decisions if you are incapacitated has ready access to these documents, as well as the loved one named in the document as the decision maker. Absent this legal directive, a hospital or healthcare facility may not have the legal authority to make these decisions solely upon consultation with family members, and the prolonged decision making and cost of providing ongoing life support and care to a loved one who would have preferred to be allowed to die naturally—could have devastating financial consequences.

4. Buy long-term care insurance immediately. It costs less when you're younger and healthier. The only exceptions are: If you have so few assets and income that you know you'll be using Medicaid and spending down 99 percent of your assets if you need long-term care; if you have enough net worth and can afford the quality of long-term care that you wish; and that you have no children, no other living relatives, no charitable interests to leave funds to at your death.

5. Put an estate plan into effect for control purposes. Available under the laws of most states, a variety of mechanisms can provide varying degrees of predictability and control to the stewardship of your assets in the event of a life crisis, health crisis, or death. These mechanisms run the gamut from the simple to the complex and labyrinthine. It is important to consult with a good estate planning attorney to evaluate your options, and select a method that works for you. One of the most common of these

devices is the revocable living trust. State laws vary, but in general, to fulfill the terms of a simple will, there is much greater ease of access for beneficiaries and greater avoidance of the expense, delay, and public record of proceeding, through the probate court. Revocable living trusts have specific purposes, but are sometimes promoted by unscrupulous folks especially in states like Florida, Arizona, and California with large aging populations so they can supposedly save on taxes. Except for those with a net worth of greater than the federal estate tax threshold—$5.34 million in 2014—or double if married, possible tax savings from revocable trusts are negligible—depending on how much is in your estate and your state laws.

The real benefit of the revocable trust is the avoidance of probate. More complex trusts can be created to provide more control, and importantly, a trust will give control of your assets to a trustee, in the event of a crisis. Appoint a trustee you can confide in and who understands your values and intentions. It is also critical to appoint a successor trustee in case something happens to the primary trustee. Although more complex, consider making the trust the beneficiary of "beneficiary-driven" assets such as life insurance, annuities, IRAs, 401(k)s. IRAs, and other retirement plans can not be owned by a trust. A good trust can also help protect assets so that they stay in your family in the event of a child's divorce, and, perhaps, help prevent the inadvertent disinheritance of grandchildren.

6. Have a pour-over will. Do you need both a will and a trust? Yes, both are important just in case there is something left out of the trust that pops up and you don't want it to go through probate court. A pour-over will is typically set up by someone who has established a trust. This stipulates that upon the death of that individual, all of her assets are to be transferred or "poured over" to the trust.

7. Make a master financial list (what many professionals term a "Survivors' Guide") of what you own and where everything is kept. Do this again both on paper and digitally. I had to search for the safe-deposit box keys, keys to two locked boxes, and more. I found these in a drawer after digging through Nolan's 45 pairs of socks and multiple pairs of underwear.

8. Keep a master list of doctors and passwords. I could not get into my husband's work/home computer. I didn't know the password for his phone. I tried guessing; nothing worked. Finally, I called his company and someone there was able to track down his password. Also, store online and in a master list access codes, personal ID numbers, the combinations to your home alarm, safe, where spare keys are kept. All of the above can and should go into a comprehensive Survivors' Guide.

9. Gather other pertinent financial data. If your husband has a 401(k), pension, nonqualified deferred compensation, stock options, or any money coming to him from the company for which he works or where he's a partner or shareholder, it's important to have names, numbers, and e-mails of those in the company's Human Resources department to track down this information. I had to make several phone calls to learn what Nolan was due.

10. Have a list of all credit cards and important documents. These include mortgage papers, passport, savings bonds, stock certificates, cemetery plots. Again, all should be on another master paper and digital list.

11. Store everything safely. Purchase a fire- and waterproof home safe where you can store documents and any jewelry that require ready access, or make use of the safe-deposit box you may be paying an annual fee to maintain, and keep documents there.

12. Make photocopies and digital photocopies (scans) for extra safety. You'll want copies of favorite family photographs, important papers, insurance policies, Social Security cards, all your lists of valuables. Consider storing them at an off-site location such as a safe-deposit box.

13. Share the information with your confidantes. Tell your attorney, financial advisor, trustees, durable power holders, and your children where everything is located. Also, e-mail a list of all critical items to these contacts, so they'll know the location once you die or become incapacitated.

14. Inventory belongings. This is a good idea because of natural disasters, fires, thefts. Do so with digital photos or a video recording. It also helps if you want to sell your home. Make a written list or do so on the computer room by room. Inventory all possessions and include serial numbers, purchase dates, and prices of

valuable belongings and updated appraisals. Update these lists yearly. E-mail the digital photographs to yourself to have them safely "in the cloud."

15. Keep portable file boxes in a safe place for tax records and other paper work. Mark the tops and sides of boxes and files with the contents. Store the boxes where they are accessible, but in a location that is dry, not in a potentially wet basement. I kept them in an upstairs closet, but had to wade through piles of clothes and junk to find them.

16. Store and back up computer data on an external hard drive. For extra safety, store this also in the cloud by scanning and e-mailing to yourself.

17. Make an appointment for a face-to-face meeting with a Social Security employee. Be prepared to wait, but you'll age less than if you wait on the phone. I know. You are entitled to your deceased husband's Social Security if he is eligible for these benefits. To collect his full Social Security benefit, you must have reached your full retirement age, although you can get reduced benefits for yourself starting at age sixty, or age fifty if you are disabled and unmarried. You may have to pay federal income taxes on these benefits if you have other substantial income such as wages, self-employment, interest, or dividends, in addition to your benefits. If you are under age sixty-six or full retirement age, it might be in your best interest to defer any Social Security income until then. This is a complex topic, so discuss it with your financial professional.

18. Meet regularly with your financial planner, if you use one—at least once a year or more if you have concerns. Talk about your level of risk tolerance since it may change. Challenge the advisor. Discuss how your portfolio is doing. It's your money and your future. You can change course. Do your research and have a list of questions when you meet each time such as, "How am I doing against my original plan?" "Here's what's been happening in my life. Should we make a change?" "Is there anything else I should be doing financially to meet my goals and also be safe?" Remember, you are not locked into your original plan and even this relationship. Speak up and resolve any concerns.

19. If your income requires, discuss with your CPA or accountant the importance of paying quarterly estimated taxes. The income plan should include: Social Security, pension (perhaps from your late husband), IRA ongoing payments, annuity payments, and others. You don't want to discover that your April 15th payment gives you sticker shock. Paying quarterly estimated payments, if your income taxes are expected to go up, will minimize that big, fat number.

If your planner does a good job with you as copilot, you'll find yourself at the point where I now am now treating myself to massages and pedicures, and indulging my biggest splurges of occasionally heading to my favorite book, wine, and food stores.

Getting a House in Order

Nolan's death was unexpected, but his long illness might have pushed others to get their financial house in order sooner than I did. When Sue W.'s husband died of throat cancer four years ago, she found herself in dire financial straits. She had tried to plan well, just in case, although both were in denial that death was imminent. She did all the bill paying, but money was always tight. "I am still just scraping by," she said. During his five-year illness, her husband continued to work construction jobs in between surgeries, but in 2009, he lost his job and was deeply depressed. Of course, their income went down considerably. Sue, a graphics designer, also had a financial hit in her profession. The field was shifting and shrinking. She was making about one-fourth of her previous salary and had to augment her paltry income moonlighting as a salesperson at Walmart.

When her husband died, she collected life insurance that barely covered three years of large house payments. She refinanced the house that reduced her payments $400 a month and got a HARP loan. HARP targets borrowers with loan-to-value ratios equal to or greater than 80 percent and who have limited delinquencies over the twelve months prior to refinancing. Through HARP, the borrower who has little to no equity can refinance without new or additional mortgage insurance, get a lower interest rate (which means less out-of-pocket costs each month), a shorter loan term, or change from an adjustable to fixed-rate mortgage. There's no minimum credit score needed.

The HARP loan has enabled Sue to hang on to her home. Her parents have offered to lend her money to make any house payments she can't meet. Recently, she went to real estate school to get her license and just started selling residential properties but noted, it takes a while to get established in the business. And, her income from real estate is based on the commission from sales. She is finally starting to sell some properties with hopes of hanging on to the home she and her late husband built.

BARBARA

LOOKING FOR FIRM FINANCIAL FOOTING

During the long process of getting divorced and afterward, I struggled to find financial terra firma. I was having nightmares about all the money going down the drain, the abrupt change in my financial status, and my uncertain emotional future. My daughters tried to do their part to avoid asking me for extra funds; one took a small job at college life guarding and also working sporadically in a coffee shop; the other baby-sat for some professors' kids at her university. I was touched, but emphasized that extra time was for studies and fun; we would manage and still be a family, just a new version.

I had never considered myself indulgent with clothing, jewelry, and cars. My passions had been travel, furniture, and art for our home—and occasionally a special meal out. I knew I had to pull in the reins, even after selling my house and renting for a few years. I also learned during the process on my own and from experts I hired what I should have done before, which would help me advise friends who started to ask for themselves and friends of friends going through divorce and widowhood. All of a sudden I was considered the expert. "Ask Barbara," I kept hearing, which at least made me laugh. Here's what I learned:

A good financial advisor can help your divorce lawyer evaluate the tax attributes of your holdings and help decide upon an approach to the division of your assets and establishing levels of ongoing financial support. Here are some things to consider asking for in your divorce, though you're not likely to get all of them and some of them may only be available in certain circumstances such as a negotiated settlement other than by a court order after a trial:

- Alimony, including a cost of living (COLA) increase so your purchasing power doesn't decrease yearly. This is something that may be negotiated in an agreed-upon settlement, although it may not be possible under your state's law for the court to order it in a trial.
- Life insurance you purchase and own on your ex to cover alimony in case of his death. What's the good of alimony if he walks out of the courtroom post decree and gets hit by a bus? Try to have the court require him to be the insured.
- Disability insurance to protect your alimony from his disability and/or incapacity. Again, it is unlikely that your judge can order this in a trial, but it is certainly something that can be negotiated for in a settlement.
- Your own long-term care insurance—the sooner the better, since costs increase with age and health problems and you want coverage for as long as you can obtain it. Again, this is not likely something your judge can order in a trial, but is something that can be negotiated for in a settlement.
- Health insurance, particularly after COBRA ends and if Medicare hasn't kicked in—with major catastrophes covered. Seek as low a monthly premium as possible, few co-pays or no co-pays, a good drug plan, and the option to choose the best doctors and hospitals.
- An equitable share in your spouse's pension funds.
- A payment in exchange for your marital share of the value of a family business if he's an owner or shareholder, or other comparable assets.
- Furnishings that you love and purchased, but be prepared to divide other shared possessions.
- School tuitions and any summer programs that have been in place, or that you can negotiate.
- Funds for the kids' upcoming weddings, Bar and Bat Mitzvahs, communions, sweet sixteen parties, graduations, college and graduate school, or any big expenses, so you don't have to engage in

disagreements over who pays for the band, flowers, cake, gown, and so on while you are walking your child down the aisle. This is not something the court may likely order, but it is something that can be negotiated in a settlement.

- Social Security benefits if your former husband is eligible, since under federal law you can receive spousal benefits on his work record, even if he remarries. But you must have been married to him for at least ten years and remain unmarried in most cases. When you hit the age when you want to start collecting your own—sixty-seven, sixty-eight, sixty-nine, seventy—you can choose either to collect a benefit up to 50 percent of his or all of yours, whichever amount is higher. If your former husband is deceased and you remain unmarried and/or old enough, you can collect all of his or all of yours, whichever is higher. Social Security laws change periodically, so be sure you talk to a professional.

Be proactive about shared funds. The moment an almost-ex says, "The passion's gone, I'm outta here," head to your attorney's office or e-mail and ask to freeze all funds, both shared and separate. This will stop removal of any 401(k) funds he's in charge of, as well as any other monies such as bank accounts in his name. If removal happens, you can still get your portion back, but that will cost legal fees and lots of hassle and heartburn.

Never comingle inherited assets. State laws vary on this, so see a lawyer in your state before proceeding. Typically, however, these assets are yours unless you combine them inadvertently, or you put the funds in joint names with your spouse, or because you didn't know, and then they may become marital or community property to be divided. Any inherited funds should be isolated from all your other assets and held in its own account. Check with a divorce lawyer as well as a trusts and estate lawyer in your state before receiving an inheritance to see how it should be held and titled in order to protect it from becoming part of the marital or community estate. It might be better to inherit funds through a trust. Inheriting an IRA can be good, but complex. Check with a professional to apprise you of the rules regarding taxes.

Get the best lawyers you can afford whether from a private firm or a legal-aid type service. This is not a place to shop price, any more than you shop price for a surgeon to perform a dangerous medical procedure. Even though it may be costly, it's worthwhile since your divorce is equivalent to the breakup of a business. This is primarily an economic transaction. You have one chance to get this right. Most women still suffer when divorced from someone in a more lucrative career. The numbers make that clear. Research has estimated that one in five women fall into poverty as a result of a divorce. That wasn't going to happen, but I was very much aware that fair does not mean equal. "Midwestern Rob," a smart attorney I met online, thought I should have selected a boutique firm with business and trial lawyers with some matrimonial or domestic experience; however, "some matrimonial or domestic experience" is not enough.

Divorce law is highly specialized, just as any other area of legal practice. Case decisions, which come down from the appellate courts every week, expand, contract, alter, or otherwise interpret the scope and application of the applicable statutes and rules. Your divorce is not a case for a "dabbler"—that is, someone who handles the occasional divorce. Rather, you want a lawyer known to the domestic relations judges as an authority and specialist. But finding any lawyer may take time due to potential conflicts. If you ask enough people in similar socioeconomic circles as yourself, you will find that in whatever city you are in the "top" names bubble to the surface, and you will begin to hear the same name or names over and over. Reputation is important! While many methods of alternate dispute resolution exist—such as negotiation, mediation, and collaborative practice—it is advisable to select an attorney whose trial ability is highly regarded. Odd as it may seem, the more capable the attorney in a trial, the less likely a trial may be necessary.

Once you have your list of candidates, cross-check these names with peer-review credentials such as membership in the American Academy of Matrimonial Lawyers (www.aaml.org), or inclusion in "Best Lawyers in America" (www.bestlawyers.com) and "Super Lawyers" (www.superlawyers.com), all in the field of family law. If the names you secure are also located in all of these references, it is a good bet that your prospective lawyer is highly competent and well respected. The state bar association can confirm that your lawyer's license is in good standing, if you are concerned.

Research in advance what a good divorce attorney does. Questions to ask include:

- Do you have time to deal with my case and me?
- Will you return phone calls or e-mails within 24 hours?
- How is the work allocated within your practice among you, associates, and paralegals?
- Will you charge me for Xeroxing, stenographers' fees, and so on?
- What percentage of cases have you settled rather than taken to trial?
- Will you give me a cell number to reach you?

Know in advance to watch costs and speak up when you think any are excessive. Don't feel intimidated by attorneys, even tough-seeming ones. On the other hand, don't think for a moment they've become your friends. Your relationship with your attorney is a professional, business relationship; this relationship is how your lawyer makes a living. You're on the same team temporarily, but you won't become long-term buddies in most cases. This is important because you are paying for competent, objective advice and advocacy, not a cheerleader or pal. The lawyer you select should be willing to share bad news with you and give you candid advice, even if you don't really want to hear it.

- **Update your will.** You want to be sure not to leave all to your almost-ex by mistake, especially in case something happens to you before the decree is finalized. That means also updating all the beneficiaries on pensions, annuities, and life insurance plans. After changing beneficiaries, be sure to get a copy of each beneficiary form and safeguard these just as you do a will—with your attorney and in a safety deposit box. If you don't have a will, get one written fast.
- **Don't give up anything in advance.** If he says he's taking to his new home the watercolor painting you purchased together on your honeymoon since the colors match his new honey's eyes, stand firm. If he also wants the outdoor wicker furniture, again explain he'll have to wait until the lawyers or court divide assets, or the two of you can decide together who gets what. In the meantime, dig out all original bills and have everything appraised by a member of an accredited appraisal organization for current values, and list (with proof) any furnishings you inherited.

- Don't move out of your house under any condition. Even if that means setting up a Maginot Line and designating times you each use the kitchen, learn to cope if he refuses to leave. One couple I know did that in their apartment. If he really wants out of the marriage and suggests moving out, encourage him to pack. But again, don't allow him to take anything important.
- Get copies of everything you can. You should have all documents copied in a safe place even in the happiest of marriages, but you definitely need them for a divorce—copies of his firm assets (especially a partnership or family business), cell phone calls, travel records, charge accounts, wills of family members, and so on. Search through drawers, his briefcase, suit pockets. This is no longer a time to ask first and be polite. Once you have copies of everything, scan them and e-mail them to yourself and your attorney. Keep that e-mail in a "Save Folder" as backup, so that you can get at it quickly should you need it.
- Be sure you co-own the house, cars, boats, and other important assets. You never know if he might trade in any possessions without asking and buy a new, cute car, motorcycle, or boat.
- Be a good detective when you must. Nobody wants to be suspicious, but certain behaviors should make you take note something is up and not just a fleeting midlife crisis. Lifetime TV shows will give you lots of storylines that may mirror reality—a new hair style; spiffier leather clothing when he's never been a biker; loss of weight; new exercise regimen; new sporty car; flowers or jewelry sent to someone other than the wife (both happened to women I know), but with bills inadvertently landing in the family mailbox or inbox (this, too, occurred with a friend); greater use of a cell phone and talking softly in the corner of a room; excuses about everything; and much more criticism of you or even excessive praise due to guilt.

If he's owner or part-owner of a "family" (privately held) business, request or have your attorney secure copies of as much documentation that exists, including, but not limited to:

- Shareholders' agreements (buy-sell agreements)
- Balance sheet

- Profit and loss statement (income statement)
- Entity tax return(s)
- Valuation document, if a valuation has ever been done, which is rare
- Bank statement(s)

Probably the most important thing: if the family business interest will be a substantial portion of any ultimate divorce settlement, make sure your advisors, including attorney, financial advisor, and accountant (forensic), all have family business experience.

What you should know in hindsight: Divorce decisions may not please you 100 percent. You must be prepared to compromise. It is unlikely that everything will go your way in the process. Your ultimate goal should be to get as good a settlement as you can but not expect everything you hoped to receive. If you can mediate, congratulate yourself; you'll have more money for later. Rather than have a trial judge make decisions, if you can settle, you're also more likely to get more of what you want. Many judges try to be fair and equal to avoid appeals. Know in advance that attorneys can become competitive. Some are working to promote their reputations and secure another win for their belts. Getting a lump sum rather than alimony is smart since it won't keep you tethered to your former spouse, if you have fewer assets and less income than he does. One date wisely advised me as my case dragged on: "End this as soon as you can or else we'll be talking about this next year and the year after." I listened and tried. In some cases, a judge may neglect making all necessary decisions; perhaps because the court system is overloaded or they're so tired of your case and eager to end it. You may have to resolve some issues in those cases, but try to let some go. And even when you think it's over, either side can file an appeal, which means more funds, more time, more heartache remembering, and more delays with getting on with your new life. Know in advance that most appeals courts leave in place a trial judge's decision. It's rare that any issues will be overturned, unless legal or factual errors were made. The standard of appellate review is that the trial court has discretion, unless it didn't consider the evidence properly or made a decision that was so contrary to the evidence that it abused its discretion.

In my case, the end was in sight four years after the separation, much too long a period. But the good news was that I stopped having so many nightmares, my blood pressure decreased, and I was delighted to take total blame as well as credit for all my actions, heave a huge sigh of relief, and start to move on. Friends who owned a vacation condo gave me the best closing present: a week at their home with anyone I chose to take along. My daughters and I quickly packed our bags for some much-needed relaxation.

6

YIKES! I HAVE TO DO WHAT NOW

MARGARET

ON MY OWN

I was sitting on the basement floor sorting my two sons' thousands of baseball cards into categories by teams while munching on a turkey and Swiss cheese sandwich when I spied it out of the corner of my eye. A large black hairy spider was creeping across the floor and headed in my direction. I felt my breath catch, my heart race; I jumped up and shrieked, "Help!" I have no idea whom I was calling out to since I was completely alone.

After spewing a string of expletives that included, "Nolan; how could you leave me like this?" I expected him to answer and maybe show up. I realized my only option was to go into attack mode. I removed one heavy sneaker and while yelling, "Yuck, yuck," I scrunched the creature in a paper towel, and made a beeline for the trash can. I shut the lid fast so no oxygen could get in to save it. It was one more reminder, albeit a small one, that I was really on my own.

I didn't expect to become a widow so young, at age sixty-four. How could this have happened to me? My parents were still married, my mother in her late eighties and my father ninety-two; my father-in-law died at age eighty-five, but my mother-in-law was ninety-five and going strong. Nolan and I had each begun thinking of retiring and traveling, now that our three children were adults and supporting themselves. These were going to be our payoff years, having happily spent forty-two years together. I certainly didn't think I'd end up alone.

Because two of my three children lived out of town, as did all three of my siblings, I had to proceed on my own—a first, since I married straight out of college. Other than writing, a very private career, I had placed myself in a subordinate position and fit like a puzzle piece into Nolan's life of music, entertaining, and wine. I wasn't an anomaly. That's what many women did at the time. Born in the 1940s and raised in the '50s and '60s, I was part of the female generation who was brought up to make as good a marriage as possible, as early as possible, leave the workforce or work part-time from home, and care for families and homes. Sheryl Sandberg's concept of leaning in was nowhere on the horizon.

My husband had been my rock. He was Humphrey Bogart to my Katherine Hepburn in one of our favorite movies, *African Queen*— the captain of our ship. There was something deeply charming, almost re-freshing, about his unabashed conventionality. In return for the security and protection he provided, I offered intimacy, children, and manage-ment of the household, the inside person who cooked, baked, did laun-dry, vacuumed, washed dishes, cared for the kids, cleaned up messes, drove carpool, walked the dog, and even helped care for his mother, with whom I had a good relationship. I was also the community volun-teer—serving on the PTA and becoming a friend at a hospital, the art museum, and symphony. Of course, there was love, companionship, and lots of laughs between us, but we each played parts in a traditional division of labor that reflected gender roles of our era.

Throughout our years together, there was an unspoken, but ac-cepted list of things I didn't do and thought I'd never have to do:

- Plunge toilets
- Unclog pipes
- Clean the swimming pool, especially if creatures floated in it
- Mulch, mow, aerate, or plant grass seed
- Trim bushes
- Fix or hook up anything technological, especially computers, TV devices, sound systems
- Use a chain saw or any tool

- Glue and fix broken items
- Mix drinks
- Open wine bottles
- Buy his and hers cemetery plots
- Host a dinner party solo
- Deal with the death of his mother
- Deal with moving my parents to a senior community and then moving my mother subsequently to an extended-care facility
- Buy two for one vitamins at Walgreens
- Join a Y, rather than a fancy gym, for yoga
- Go to social events alone at night and drive myself in the dark
- Sell an antique, stick-shift car
- Date again
- Craft a new life

On the other hand, my husband never

- washed a dish;
- cleaned the kitchen or wiped up crumbs;
- vacuumed (he was good at picking up his feet so I could vacuum under them);
- did laundry, except once, when he shrunk a dress to a child's size;
- cleaned a closet, drawer, basement, attic, or garage (I knew he didn't have an affair during our marriage for if he had, I would have found evidence since he NEVER threw anything away—no travel or jewelry receipts or long, cell phone bill.);
- baked;
- ate leftovers.

There was also a list of tasks my husband thought he could do much better than I could do:

- Budget and prepare taxes
- Fill a gas tank and do maintenance on the car
- Balance the family checkbook
- Deal with tradespeople and financial experts
- Haggle with car dealers
- Negotiate with airline clerks and hotel employees for a better seat and flight or an upgraded room

- Fix plumbing
- Hang pictures
- Hook up a washer and dryer
- Stain floors
- Paint walls and spray paint cabinets and furniture
- Power spray the patio
- Fertilize and trim bushes, mow the lawn and rake
- Clip coupons and find great deals for dinners and movies

And then, he was gone, leaving me feeling like an adolescent who wished she could be handier, and tougher, as well as prettier, taller, bustier, more popular, and adept at mingling alone. Since I was far from an adolescent with teenage dreams and fantasies, I tried a more rational approach. I decided faith might help, but most important would be the philosophy that perseverance could change consciousness. What I thought, could become possible. I heard that somewhere.

Yet, I was still confused about my new role. I had played Nolan's wife for so long, it defined who I was. How did I fit into society? Would I still have the same friends, most of whom were couples? Would I meet new people? Would I have to hang out with other single women most of the time? Would I ever want to date? Find someone who was handy? How would I navigate a world where social interaction meant Internet dating, going on Facebook, tweeting, and texting? Most of all I wondered how would I get undressed again and have sex with someone other than my husband!

Man up Margaret, I said to myself. There are real problems in the world; yours are fairly inconsequential at this point. I did what I always did when I hit a wall. I went into action. I was still working full-time and that was good because it was part of the old routine.

I needed therapy desperately. I met with a psychologist who specialized in grief. Some of our sessions went like this: "When will I feel better? Every time the phone rings, I think it's my husband. I keep expecting him to come through the door. Is that normal?" To which she responded, "Get to a grief support group and learn what others are going through." It would, she said, help me determine what the grieving process was all about.

The group was a godsend. What a relief to hear that I wasn't the only kook who expected her spouse to return miraculously. Each person in my group had a story with a common thread. Robin who slept with her husband's ashes and moved them from room to room; Lauren whose daughter felt it was her mother's fault their father died because she didn't get him to the hospital fast enough, or Mary who turned to God for comfort. I was ready to write a sitcom.

And then slowly one by one, we all started to feel better and empowered. Each of us realized we could make it on our own. Natalie fell in love with someone at work; Lauren became a grandmother and that helped repair the relationship with her daughter; Mary was still into God but found a man to date at her church. Thank you, God. We continued to get together to celebrate life rather than death.

As for me, I let go of my fantasy that Nolan would be back and life would resume as it had been. In the interim, there were many things I learned to master. I started paying attention to my investments, collected my husband's Social Security, got ready to sell our house and many of its contents, moved to a condominium my family owned, hired caregivers for my mom (repeatedly when they quit for a variety of reasons or we let them go) and found new doctors for her, and even met and made new friends. On the phone, I also learned to understand technical people with their thick foreign accents, and stopped being impatient with them. Most important, I began to create a new life once I accepted that being Nolan's wife was very important, but just a small piece of who I was.

Today, I say with pride, I can

- turn off water if there's a leak (I now know where the main valve is, too);
- pay bills (some online) and balance a checkbook;
- deal with tradespeople calmly;
- negotiate the sale of an item;
- sit down and make investment decisions with a financial professional, including how I want to leave my money;
- sell a house on my own—getting it cleaned out and ready for sale;
- throw a great formal dinner party and uncork the wine, after selecting good ones; .
- plan my own trips and travel alone;
- drive on icy dark roads at night using my GPS or asking Siri for directions;

- purge my surroundings and create order in my life;
- cook for one, two, or more;
- subscribe to publications I love, including a national daily news-paper;
- date and enjoy it—and yes, that, too.

And no longer do I have to plunge toilets, ream out drains, drag hoses around to water the lawn, shovel a driveway, plant flowers, reset the alarm, or worry about sitting home and waiting for a FedEx. I now live in a safe, well-run condo building where I can walk to the desk in the lobby and pick up a package for which they've signed or pick up the phone and say, "Ann, my water heater is leaking. Can you send some-one up to look at it?"

I probably still will never feel comfortable hanging pictures or a light fixture, cleaning out an attic, using a chain saw, or laying tile, but I have cultivated a list of experts, friends, and family who can change a shower-head, hook up a computer or printer and fix them if there's a glitch, set up my new coffee machine, and figure out the router for my broad-band. I am finally comfortable putting out framed photos of Nolan, which at first I was loathe to do. I didn't need photos; his memory is lodged deeply within me without having to display it.

If nothing else, I've had many laughs, fewer crying jags, and good stories to share with my children. Now, on many days, I walk to the front desk of my condo building, catching the eye of the concierge on duty who laughs and asks, "What now?" What a relief that on most days I can walk by briskly and respond, "Absolutely nothing. I'm only headed out to take a walk by myself." And I've even learned to love walking alone and being alone, too—at times.

BARBARA

SOLO GIG

Even though my family home seemed too large, empty, and quiet once I was separated, I thought it important to stay put to provide the root-edness both daughters seemed to need. Doing so also gave me a semblance of continuity as our family of four dissolved. I was terrified as my younger daughter got ready to leave for college. I would then really be alone.

My daughters were nervous, too, about how I would survive. They had always been impressed with my cooking, ability to entertain effortlessly, ability to work hard from a home office and not be distracted by daytime TV, doing laundry, shopping, or rooting through the contents of our refrigerator. They also shared that they thought I would make new friends. "You can talk to anyone," my older daughter said lovingly.

Yet, they worried at my inability to master certain housekeeping chores—from using the microwave (which I had never felt I needed), to ironing (a skill belonging to my former husband) and dusting (anathema to my gene pool). Before each girl departed, they urged me also to become less intimidated by all the rapid changes in computer technology. "Try, play around, you'll be better than you think," my younger daughter advised, though I knew she had serious doubts. My older daughter, more blunt with her consoling, was incredulous, though I knew it was from love, "Mom, how can you be so clueless about this stuff?"

The girls joked, though I felt deep down they were serious, as they debated rotating staying at home instead of simultaneously attending their different colleges miles apart from home. My younger daughter was most concerned that I'd forget to turn off the oven or snuff out a flame. "Mom, put sticky notes everywhere," she suggested, as tears welled in her eyes. My older daughter worried that I would forget to use the lineup of skin-care products she had purchased for me and follow the regimen she wrote and posted on my bathroom wall. Her goal was to slow any marks of aging. She had begun to accept that I would be divorced, but not that I might look old, too.

Even my then eighty-three-year-old widowed mother was afraid I'd forget to restock the refrigerator and pantry in case of a storm, as she always did. We used to joke she could feed an army if one showed up, and even have leftovers for them to pack. She also suggested we move in together to forestall loneliness, which she knew all too much about, having lost my father eleven years before.

I rationalized out loud with my daughters that being alone was an important lesson for me to master, even at my advanced age. I remember saying, "No life remains unscathed if you are fortunate to live long enough. You may not get the best roommates or classes after 10 a.m., but such glitches are bound to be temporary, and you'll survive. I'll survive this, too."

The reality of living alone proved much harder for me than having a pipe burst in the cold and knowing whom to call and how to clean up the mess, or deciding what car to buy when mine hit the 130,000-mile mark and started having problems. Friends, including Nolan, were eager to offer input. Even my lawyer, who owned a Porsche, weighed in. "Buy something cute you'll love. Now is the time," he advised. Like Margaret, I had never lived alone except for my freshman year in college. Yes, I had flown to a foreign country when I was thirteen years old for a summer program, but that was then when I was young. I had been a part of a couple for so long I didn't know what it was like to come home to a dark house late at night, grocery shop for one, take a shower without anybody in the house (I had seen *Psycho* too many times), or walk into a party on my own, begin a conversation, and then move on to another person when someone seemed uninterested in me, turned away, or gave some lame excuse. "Oh, there's so-and-so. We have to catch up." I tried not to take it personally, though initially I did.

I knew I wasn't the only woman my age going through this and living alone. However, it wasn't until years later I learned that academics studied folks like Margaret and me. We at least represented good guinea pigs. Rebecca K. Ratner, professor of marketing at the Robert H. Smith School of Business at the University of Maryland in College Park, and colleague Rebecca W. Hamilton, professor of marketing at the McDonough School of Business, Georgetown University, wrote in "Inhibited from Bowling Alone," their article in *Journal of Consumer Research*, May 28, 2015, about experiments they conducted. They explained that people who do certain activities like going to art galleries, the movies, or eating at a restaurant may have the same degree of enjoyment whether they're alone or with others. "Consumers seem to overestimate how much their enjoyment of these activities depends on whether they are accompanied by a companion," they wrote in the paper's abstract.

For those experiments, the professors didn't study the reason but others have, Ratner explained—what's termed the "spotlight effect," a label coined first in 1998 by Kenneth Savitsky and Thomas Gilovich. In a paper Gilovich wrote with Savitsky and Victoria Husted Medvec for the *Journal of Personality and Social Psychology*, they said, "People tend to believe that more people take note of their actions and appearance than is actually the case. We dub this putative phenomenon the spotlight effect: People tend to believe that the social spotlight shines more brightly on them than it really does." And this is true in both positive and negative circumstances, and often when they're doing something alone. In that case they may feel overly self-conscious and, in fact, a "loser," which is why many avoid the situation by not pursuing activities on their own.

Both Margaret and I followed that line of reasoning and participated in ways we felt were more acceptable and less "visible" to others—going to a movie in the afternoon rather than on a Friday or Saturday night date or couple's time, or eating in out-of-the-way places where we wouldn't be recognized. Anonymity became our safety net. Then, when a bit braver, we tiptoed into trying our solo status.

I remember walking into one vintage pizza place in my neighborhood when it was almost empty midweek. I thought I would be royally welcomed as I plopped myself down in a comfy booth for four so I could spread out my newspaper. The manager came over and informed me rather rudely that he wanted to save the bigger booths for people accompanied by others. I cringed, got up and moved to a smaller booth instead of leaving or saying what I wanted to shriek: "Don't you know I've been dumped and am trying to rebuild my life? I only want one lousy slice of pizza and salad, and will eat fast." I didn't, of course, but certainly felt invisible and worthless as the fifth wheel I had become among my couple friends. Today, I would say something calmly yet firmly, and get up and leave. Then, I didn't have the chutzpah.

After that, I tried to cope better by thinking of my fantasy life as an adventure and imagine how my fictional heroines might handle similar situations. Nancy Drew would have been too busy being a young sleuth to worry. Jessica Fletcher in *Murder, She Wrote* was so interesting everyone wanted to be her friend and hear about her latest murder mystery case. And Murphy Brown, in the sitcom by that name, had the uncanny ability to strike up enduring friendships with her work crew, including her painter Eldin.

And then I filled my time by doing things I had always wanted to or felt I should if I were to write my version of *The 100 Things to Do After Your Divorce and Before You Die*: learn to swing dance, make a great cup of coffee with the ex's prize coffee maker and fresh beans; go to a movie alone on a Friday evening—Saturday was still pushing it; make my bedroom a refuge where I could read a good book; take a cupcake-making class with one daughter in order to master fondant icing for the wedding cake I would bake some day if my daughters only asked, and learn to fill in Excel spreadsheets on a computer (which I proudly mastered—with help).

At some point, probably when I had to put in a sump pump, add French drains inside and outside, and install a new roof, the house became too much of a financial albatross. I realized I was working to support my home. When my real-estate saleswoman said she had a buyer, I agreed, then found an excuse. "Their offer wasn't sufficient, and it's too early for me to leave," I explained. I was being emotional, rather than financially smart.

A year later before the market turned down prior to the recession, the real estate salesperson became more adamant: "The market's changing, and you don't need this house. Your daughters are not return-ing, and you need to get as much out of it as you can." I still balked, "I write about real estate all the time, and the market here is still strong." Yet, when the agent brought me another buyer and showed me smaller homes and even apartments, I knew it was time to agree. I began sorting through belongings—deciding what to save for myself and daughters, give away, donate to charities, and sell through a consign-ment shop and at a yard sale. I even put out my long white wedding dress and veil, which I tagged at $35. Neither daughter wanted it; they felt it would be bad karma. But somebody bought it for her daughter to play dress-up games.

I moved into an affordable two-bedroom rental while I decided where to go permanently. Months later, I remained stuck, in part be-cause my life as a freelance writer permitted me to work anywhere as long as I had my cell phone and laptop. I debated whether to

- buy another home in this city;
- move back to the bigger midwestern city where I once lived and where I still had friends and regular work assignments;
- head east where both daughters had settled and where my aging mom lived;

- be really gutsy, put all my stuff into storage, and do what I had always yearned to do—live for several months as an ex-pat writer in some romantic, cheap, garret apartment in Paris or London.

I knew the last was a pipe dream. I could never be so selfish at this stage with my mother and daughters desperately needing me. Or maybe the truth was—I needed them too much to be so far away.

A close friend who had become a life coach urged me to close my eyes and imagine what the return address on a letterhead read. I did, and the space turned up blank. I did the next best thing and tried out other cities temporarily during my dating frenzy. One southern city with beautiful leafy suburbs, restaurants with fried green tomatoes on every other menu, and residents who spoke in a charming slow drawl made me feel uncomfortable. I felt I needed my passport to enter this foreign country equivalent, and too many I met had such completely different (conservative) political beliefs. When honest with myself, I also knew that to move and be so far from my daughters and mother would require being head over heels in love. I wasn't.

When my daughters and mom urged me to move back east and a few childhood and college friends joined the chorus, I knew the direction I was headed. I still wasn't sure of the exact place, but I would try life again on a temporary basis near my roots. I needed to know if I could handle the faster pace, greater expense, louder noises, and crowds after more than three decades in the Heartland. I had taken on a midwestern mindset. I was on my way, a pioneer. And rather than going west, I was headed in the other direction.

REFERENCES

Gilovich, T., Savitsky, K., & Medvec, V. H. 1998. "The Illusion of Transparency: Biased Assessments of Others' Ability to Read One's Emotional States." *Journal of Personality and Social Psychology* 75 (2): 332–46. doi: 10.1037/0022-3514.75.2.332. Retrieved July 20, 2011.

Ratner, Rebecca K., and Hamilton, Rebecca W. 2015. "Inhibited from Bowling Alone." *Journal of Consumer Research*. First published online: May 28. DOI: http://dx.doi.org/10.1093/jcr/ucv012 ucv012.

7

HOME SWEET HOME?

MARGARET

FINDING A NEW ADDRESS

It was the winter of 2013, nearly two years after my husband passed away, and time at last to sell the home where we had lived for 37 years and raised our children. Not only was my house too large just for me and becoming a money pit—breaking down like a body in old age, but walking into an empty home in the dead of winter at night was also like entering a dark dreary cave. And the house held too many memories.

Experts caution not to make any major decisions for at least a year after losing a spouse. That included any plans to sell a house. Pat E. ignored the experts and sold her beautiful suburban ranch home just three months after her husband Jim died. To add insult to injury, she bought her youngest daughter's rundown bungalow in the city. "She had put it on the market. It wasn't selling. I didn't want her to be unhappy because she had just lost her father. So I told her if it didn't sell, I would buy it. It was a rash and impulsive decision."

Pat's nice house sold quickly, and she moved into the bungalow. "By the time I sat down and surveyed the home, I was hit by a bolt of lightning. I was stuck with this huge problem of a house that I had to remodel if I had any hope of selling it and getting out. Initially, I hardly got out of bed; I cried all the time," she recalls.

Financially and emotionally, she says, it was a disaster. "I sold a really nice house and got a good price for it, bought the bungalow, and ended up sinking money into repairing it that I'll never recoup. I will probably lose at least $40,000 when I sell. The remodeling, at least, will make it more saleable," she rationalizes. Her advice in hindsight: "After Jim died, I felt like I was in a trance. I wasn't making good decisions about anything. Be as patient as you can be and don't be influenced by anyone. You have to think of yourself and your own emotional and financial future." Pat plans to put the bungalow on the market as soon as she knows where she wants to live next.

I was ready to sell. My husband and I had made all decisions together. But it was time to do so alone. Friends offered to help, but I felt I had to tackle this on my own initially. To get the house ready for listing meant cleaning and clearing it out, then hiring the right work staff to tackle repairs, which we had neglected during Nolan's multiple illnesses. The market had also softened, and the inventory that sold for the highest price fastest was in pristine condition. Buyers had become incredibly picky. Our house wasn't for those wanting a perfect chef's kitchen; huge walk-in closets; drop-dead, magazine-style yard; and spa bathroom, though we did have the whirlpool we rarely used. We had loved our house, but I was ready to let it go.

I gathered names of contractors and interviewed three, totally aware that a single woman would be an open invitation to be taken advantage of. Barbara had taken this step first and guided me about getting at least three bids. The initial candidate was too expensive. Had he ever heard of cut-rate? I told him in no uncertain terms that I was moving and didn't care to use expensive, imported Italian marble for kitchen countertops or equally pricey French bathroom fixtures. Home Depot's and Lowe's basic merchandise would suffice. This wasn't about decorating for my taste, but staging to sell—and the quicker the better.

The second contractor, a man I had used before to cosmetically tweak our kitchen and master bath, took advantage of my new status: the dreaded *W*, as in widow. He spent one hour talking to me about the benefits of Testosterone cream! Although he'd probably work quickly with his elevated, energetic T-levels, I nixed him out of fear that I wouldn't be able to get him out of my house at the end of the workday.

I ended up hiring a woman who talked tough and was smart. She alluded to her family's mob connections in Chicago, and I felt if something went wrong, she'd have the right people to take out any person who crossed me. I almost considered using that card when dealing with the trash company that complained it couldn't lift my overstuffed garbage cans—and then charged me extra for doing so. "Have you ever heard of putting them on a dolly?" I asked. They reluctantly reduced the bill, and I realized I had more moxie than I thought.

Before I could tackle the fix up, I had to face the dreaded clean up. My real estate saleswoman kept advising me: "Make it look larger by getting it empty; every closet should look half full; every countertop must only display three items." Our basement was the exact opposite; it resembled a waste dump. Nolan couldn't bear to part with anything. A small narrow pathway from the steps to the laundry equipment was flanked by floor-to-ceiling, old, cardboard boxes he had saved in case something had to be returned. This included the original cartons for our 25-year-old microwave and 20-year-old TV.

Additionally, there were two or three Weedwackers and exercise equipment, the kind advertised on TV at 2 a.m. by Ronco; and four sets of garish, cheesy, gold flatware made in Taiwan that I gave to a good friend who coveted it. Her husband thought it was atrocious and checked the value online. They ended up giving it to their gardener. In addition, there were promotional liquor and wine mirrors and umbrellas, perfect for those eateries that sell wings and 30 flavors of martinis; vintage clothing from my grandmother who left behind a collection of politically incorrect fur hats; a broken VCR my husband kept having repaired, though it would have cost less each time to buy new; and a group of stringed instruments with missing strings. And that was only the beginning of his hoarding.

One of the first things I did—after asking everyone I knew if they wanted anything—was to rent a dumpster to part with stuff. Some of my furniture was too pathetic to give away. A friend of a friend came by, took one look, and laughed at the disarray. I almost sold a black leather lazy boy chair to someone's sister. She weighed nearly 300 pounds and when she tried it out, the chair tipped over and the sale was quashed, as well as her shirt that got caught in the foot foldout section.

Then, there were the books. I love books and usually have one with me before the start of a movie, but I knew I couldn't take all with me, wherever I was going, and I didn't know yet where that was. I gave thousands to Goodwill, many of which were dog eared and marked with highlighter or had scribbles in the margins such as "Wow! Great recipe" or "Hum, I should try this with my husband," or words I didn't know and their meanings such as "amanuensis," "palimpsest," and "inscrutable." Among the books I kept were classics by Austin, Dickens, and the Brontës—forever favorites. I kept some signed first editions too, written mostly by Israelis that I purchased at obligatory fundraisers, a handful of books Barbara and I had coauthored, and some written by close friends.

I also found thousands of vinyl records, family documents, baseball scorebooks since 1960, datebooks thirty and forty years old, two decades of magazines and newspapers, and hundreds of photos. In some photos, I didn't know who the people were, though countless times I've searched their faces and clothing for clues. Where are they now? I wondered. Others I knew about. The little boy who bit my youngest son in nursery school. My oldest son's childhood friend who is pictured wearing very short shorts and high white knee socks and now heads a major public relations firm and has learned to dress well. Many of my daughter's friends are pictured without makeup or pretense, and are very young—some even sport the remains of baby fat, teenage angst, and acne. Some today are actors on such TV shows as *Glee* or have roles in plays on Broadway, a career path my daughter considered but gave up to go into the wine business as her dad had done.

Troubling, however, was the great sadness I saw up close in so many other photos—the slow, steady decline of my husband and the loss of his gorgeous dark head of hair still thick in his sixties. His appearance was altered, his face haggard yet bloated from the Prednisone. The sadness wasn't just in shuffling through old photos. It came through in his other collections. No longer was there just his lineup of the best raincoats, top coats and jackets, dozens of the finest ties to reflect his good taste and interest in clothing. There was a fleet of bicycles he loved, and hundreds of miniature liquor bottles and wines from his twenty-five years of work promoting certain spirits and wines. But there were also many of his almost empty pill bottles—several of each kind— or reams of paper on which he wrote his requests to doctors and nurses, and flannel shirts I had bought to keep him warm when he had terrible chills and fever.

A high point of purging were funny moments, too, including the process of shedding my old kitchen items—the blender we fixed several times that spewed one son's green herbal smoothie goo all over our white cabinets, the toaster oven that caught fire when my husband forgot about the grilled cheese sandwich he was cooking, the TV with the fuzzy picture, dishes with cracks and chips, and our gaggle of gas station mugs from our countless road trips.

Throughout the six-month-long process, I often found myself cursing my husband for not being there to help me. I wanted to pitch everything. My well-meaning friends weighed in: "Keep it in the family" or "Dump it on your kids" was the collective response to their shock when they came in the house and saw the piles of stuff. But kids today are different. Mine aren't settled permanently in homes. They didn't want most of the remembrances. They desire new gadgets, not an antique, rusted, hand-push lawn mower; Radio Flyer wagon; old hockey skates; high school megaphone; or bandstands bearing such names as the eponymous Nolan Crane Band. All the kids ended up wanting were a few old cameras, an afghan my mother-in-law crocheted, many photos, CDs and record albums, and their collections of baseball cards, coins, sheet music, music memorabilia, and instruments.

As I looked around the basement, garage, closets, and drawers after I had cleaned or organized them, I began to feel free. That feeling grew and later became a promise of the liberation I started to believe I would feel more when the house sold. With enough possessions to stage an estate sale, a friend arranged them along the interior walls of my home like soldiers standing at attention just waiting to be plucked by the hundreds of hoarders who stood around the block in a long line one April morning. They didn't seem to understand that what they clamored to buy they, too, might some day have to dispose of when their lives might change. That was their issue, not mine.

Once my home was emptier, all the warts became more visible. It needed massive repairs so prospective buyers wouldn't walk through and run out. My contractor broke the news gently. It needed a new roof; interior and exterior paint jobs; new electrical panel, venting, and wiring; some plumbing; a relaid and tuck-pointed brick patio; a fireplace liner; rugs removed so hardwood floors could be sanded and stained; and new vanities and tiled floors. I could have sold the house in "as is" condition, but I would have received so much less. I couldn't take the chance.

Workers were in my home for weeks hammering, sawing, and sanding while they bandied about such terms as "floor joist." Every so often I could hear them yell to each other, "Get a load out of this dryer vent? Are you kidding me?" They found it hilarious that my husband did so many do-it-yourself projects, most of which he jerry-rigged and botched.

Two months after the work began, the house with its facelift—an expensive operation that cost thousands and thousands—looked 30 years younger and fresher. I didn't waver about staying, however. It was ready to go on the market. I disappeared for the open house, since I knew many friends and nosey neighbors would wander through. I didn't want to hear their comments about our taste if they disliked my living room upholstery and our outdated pool, or if the price seemed high. Yet, I craved the written feedback my real estate saleswoman provided, even though every time someone saw the house it was rated, reminding me of the comments on a school report card or recent Yelp or Airbnb review: "It shows well." "Who did those windows?" "Why is that wall there?" "It sure has possibilities, but needs too much work."

I had expected to have multiple good offers the first day. I had three, but they were so low, I felt insulted. I debated lowering the price, was determined not to, and then did what the professionals advised—lowered it about 5 percent. More weeks passed, and I was exhausted sweeping leaves and debris off the pool deck and patio; keeping the kitchen spotless, the cushions fluffed, the floors vacuumed, and a full roll of toilet paper always on each roll. Someone finally said: "We'll take this house," and offered a decent contract without too many provisos. Tired but elated, I jumped to sign and was ready to turn over the keys.

I packed my few remaining possessions into cardboard boxes, hired a mover for the furniture, including our baby grand piano, uncorked one of Nolan's favorite wines—a 1990 Dominus that was still palatable—and toasted the many happy memories of our marriage. It was time to forgive him for not being there and to move on physically and emotionally.

And it was time to share with others the secrets of how I got through a process so many others dread. Luckily, my mother offered me her condo. My parents had moved to a senior community and when they put their condo on the market, it didn't sell. I eagerly accepted her generosity knowing that living there rent free would allow me to retire from my full-time job and focus on new pursuits.

I breathed a sigh of relief once I moved into my new home and knew it would be a long time before I would move again.

Rule No. 1: Don't sell your home that first year after your spouse dies or you divorce. You might not be thinking straight and chance making a bad choice. You will know when it's the right time. Exception: If you can't afford to maintain and stay in the house.

Rule No. 2: When you are ready to sell, see if family or your closest friends want anything before it goes out the door with a stranger. Don't let your children convince you to box anything—and everything—up for when they have room; it's now or never, even if they beg you. Or put a statute of limitations on how long you'll hold on to their stuff. I put thousands of records and CDs in storage for the kids to take within five years after Nolan's death. If not, I will sell the items. Many of the albums are signed and rare, making them quite valuable.

Rule No. 3: When people say they want to pitch in, most mean it. Some really enjoy digging their hands into someone else's old stuff and finding treasures or going down memory lane with you. My feeling was: "You want it, you can have it. Take it. Get it out of here." One friend even whispered her reason for being so helpful: "Rooting through old stuff is better than sex."

Rule No. 4: Find one good friend or a maximum of two who will help you organize what's left into groupings by category on tables or blankets on the floor, clearing out what you don't want to keep, give to family or friends, donate to charity, or consign to a shop. Don't think about paybacks. This is what your closest friends want to do for you— their way of helping. One friend did the bulk of work by organizing all the stuff with me. My mother took her husband and her out for a nice dinner after the house was sold.

Rule No. 5: Looking at the total job is overwhelming. Break it down into small areas of each room. Put all the vases together, all books in one spot, all afghans on one bed. If you're going to have an estate sale later, spread out the stuff on empty shelves and around the perimeter of the emptiest room in your home. Before you toss anything, take photos or a video of items you want to remember. Also photograph your house as a memory book for you and your family. Write down any special memories connected with different items—the vase your grandmother gave you for a shower gift or the stethoscope your physician-dad shared for future grandchildren to play with.

Rule No. 6: Decide how you'll dispose of what's left that isn't going into an estate sale or your next home. Your overall objective is to get rid of stuff . . . before you move. Most moving companies calculate rates based partly on total cubic feet and also distance from the old place to the new one. There are several routes to go, and you may also make some money.

- Auction goods on eBay or sell on Craigslist.org. Check to see what similar items have sold for. If you want to use a bricks-and-mortar auction house, check out Auctionzip.com or contact a local auction house. Timing is crucial. Antiques right now have fallen out of favor with younger generations who mostly want sleek and contemporary furnishings. Consider storing good antiques, for everything is cyclical and the demand will come back.
- Consign if your town has a good shop, though it will take time to get the cash in most cases, but at least it gets stuff out of your house. If the stuff doesn't sell, usually it gets reduced on a regular basis, but that's still better than just giving it away at times.
- For the more valuable items, sell back to shops or dealers that you have used before. This strategy works best for higher-end antiques, good art, and jewelry. You might even make money if items appreciated, and you can authenticate the provenance with your original receipt and a description of what it is.
- Head to a flea market if you have lots of stuff—maybe, a collection of Fiesta dinnerware. Then, you unload all in one fell swoop, and have an enjoyable day in the country. The downside is you most likely will not get top dollar.
- Unload heavy items that aren't valuable by having them hauled away for free or a slight fee. This will help you avoid repeated trips to your town dumpster or renting a U-Haul. Hire a company like College Hunks Hauling Junk or 1-800-Got-Junk?.
- Donate for a tax deduction to sources like Goodwill or the Salvation Army. You will need to file Form 8283 with the U.S. Internal Revenue Service (IRS) if the amount of your deduction is more than $500. Use the "fair market" valuation guide from Goodwill or a similar source. You can find other charities by going online to

Stuffstop.com. Always ask for a receipt. Donating like this requires you to drag most items to your front hall or front lawn.

- Do more good by sending in your old phone, for example, to SmartphoneTradeIn.com, it will donate funds to Operation Gratitude, a nonprofit that supports U.S. military personnel. Other electronics companies partner with other charities.

- Organize that yard or estate sale. You often can do this yourself by first contacting your community to be sure it's permitted. But you'll need to set things out neatly on the lawn or tables, have a box to collect cash, and reorganize displays periodically. Or you can hire a professional who will price the items, place an ad, arrange balloons or signs to lead the way from main roads, set all up, and close it down at the end. Usually, you'll need to share 30–40 percent of proceeds, but you'll avoid having to do all the work or listening to rough comments for what you're selling, and you'll sidestep any neighborhood crowds.

Rule No. 7: Reduce by tossing broken and really outdated, nonvaluable items. It gets rid of some inventory immediately. It may be tough to let go, but what would you do with dozens of tie-dyed shirts and ripped tablecloths—unless you're into making quilts.

Rule No. 8: Bring in a professional to organize once you're done on your own, or before, if you feel overwhelmed. Someone who's accredited by the National Association of Professional Organizers or National Association of Senior Move Managers knows what sells and doesn't and how to best display stuff for potential buyers. Most charge by the hour or project and have websites to consult.

Rule No. 9: Ask a broker who knows your neighborhood to help sell your home or find the right salesperson. She (or he) will tell you what to do to make it salable, and can be honest in a gentle caring way. When a pro insists that you leave only three items on each counter or table, and your arrangement of five seems more striking, listen. That person has experience. It helps, too, if your real-estate salesperson lives nearby and can be at your house in a flash when a problem arises, to take over when the going gets rough, or to hold your hand when you need that. Mine did. And remember they can't change the market if it's terrible and make buyers materialize. It's not their fault! Know, too, that price is the great equalizer.

Rule No. 10: For things that need fixing—a microwave that doesn't work or cabinets with fronts that have become unhinged, find an expert (unless you've inherited the fix-it genes). It costs more to redo a do-it-yourself job that was botched and not up to code and will be uncovered during an inspection.

Rule No. 11: Maintain a sense of humor throughout, or try hard to find laughter in the process. Purging your home of stuff and selling it for a new beginning can actually be fun, and liberating, and allow you to go in a new design direction. But there will be painful moments for sure. Rooting through your 30–40-plus years of possessions can serve as a visual timeline of your life—gone in a flash.

Rule No. 12: Once you're moved in, settle in mentally for the long haul, even if it doesn't turn out to be long or forever, by doing the following:

- Check the Internet to get instructions on how to set up that new computer or how to operate that brand new induction range. You-Tube is also a good resource to show how to put something together or fix it. Take advantage of hotlines as well. I often felt frustrated initially and was ready to throw that new item across the room, but have learned to set up and fix some electronics myself, and it's a great feeling of satisfaction.
- Cultivate neighbors who are handy or ask permission of a friend to "borrow" her husband. Some women are handy, too, in my age group. My sister-in-law helped my brother change my shower-heads.
- Compile a list of experts and save it in a computer file or print it out and save a hard copy. Join websites such as Angie's List to find a good work crew. Get written estimates for any work done, and never pay upfront in full.
- Ask a teenager if having trouble with your smartphone. Does your computer have a virus? Does your computer keep freezing? Teens have grown up with technology, and often know more than any adult and cost far less. Don't know any? Ask friends and work colleagues if their kids are available, or call your local colleges for their help desk.

- Take classes at a junior or community college to learn how to do it yourself, from working on cars to repairing plumbing and computers. Many libraries also offer similar services for free.
- Tune into HGTV for home decorating and remodeling shows with ideas on certain tasks. They're a great way to glean tips on cheap chic.

When all your initial work is done, you've found places for your furnishings, and your electronic stuff is humming smoothly, it's time to learn something purely for you and not related to your house, car, kids, or late or former spouse. This could be playing bridge, learning digital photography, cooking, kayaking, or sometimes even the art of doing nothing and being alone. The sky's the limit, especially once you don't have to master fixing a leaky toilet.

8

IT TAKES A COMMUNITY

BARBARA

ENDING UP IN THE RIGHT HOOD

When life as a single became uncomfortable, I knew I had choices: stay put and try to expand my circle with new single friends through new activities, which I knew would be hard in my late fifties, or move and find a less tradition-bound community open to outsiders.

When my two daughters and mom, all living in the east, urged me to join them, I decided it was the best step to take. Starting over at my age seemed daunting, however, and expensive, and I feared leaving my close circle of nearby friends who had provided emotional sustenance during my rockiest period.

I always liked to know the outcome—the ending of a book—and hence my peeking at the last few pages. As a somewhat cautious person who didn't know the ending this time, the strategy called for a way to test the New York City waters by staying for long stretches at my mom's apartment. I would know soon if being there again would appeal, this time as a single. Once in New York, I joined a gym, got active at my alma mater in the city, and called friends and former business colleagues to let them know I was back to try to rebuild a social life. "Great" was the reaction, yet most days I was alone at my computer and everyone's social life didn't seem to necessitate another person, though there were a few exceptions.

My new friendships became mostly centered on shopkeepers in the neighborhood whom I saw daily. I knew the two brothers, both Vietnam veterans, who owned a small Italian deli, and learned they closed each summer for a month, so they could visit family abroad. I befriended the owner of a bakery who thought I looked terrific as I primped for my new single life. I chitchatted with the frame store owner whose daughter worked in a fancy meat business that sold only cuts with a pedigree, and I initiated conversations with others, including the nearby butcher, fishmonger, cheese store, and shoe repair owners.

Nights were lonely, however, since my mom went to bed early, and the Internet dating I had started to try rarely piqued my interest. The double Harvard whom I met for drinks at his Ivy League club sprung for wine but no more. He then rambled on about his great sex life with his former girlfriend. I couldn't wait to get away.

Friends in upstate New York urged me to consider their area. Their house on a lake became a refuge, and I tested it during all four seasons. But the four-hour trip from New York meant my family would rarely visit. The winter climate was also extremely cold, and the community lacked an interesting grocery store and independent book store that were at the top of my must-have list. It did have a good library, my third criteria.

Then, a cousin weighed in and suggested I consider her area: a small bucolic village with population of 7,000 that was touted as the crown jewel of the Hudson River Valley. It had one main traffic light, a bevy of sophisticated restaurants due to proximity to the Culinary Institute of America—the other C.I.A.—rolling farmland, lots of deer, the pedigree of the nearby late president Franklin Delano Roosevelt's birthplace and library (the first in the country), and a reputation for being open to transplants due to a wide mix of residents' demographics.

The village was also just one hour-plus from the Berkshire Mountains of Massachusetts, which I had long loved for its cultural activities; three hours from Boston where I had several friends; and was less than two hours by car or train to New York City.

My cousin, a real-estate salesperson, promised to find me a house within the village so I would feel safe as a single female with neighbors close by. And, hey, I might even meet my Sam Sheppard veterinarian as executive-cum-mom Diane Keaton had done in the movie *Baby Boom*. The idea of moving somewhere where I had no connection except one relative who was busy with her business and family seemed insane— and intimidating. Yet, when she picked me up the first time at the nearby train station to start our search, we ate at a charming trattoria where we had the best thin-crust flourless pizzas. My visceral reaction was fast and unequivocal: Hmmm, delicious food, and this place might be a possibility.

More visits gave me a sense of a community through its independent bookstore with regular readings, signings, and a book club, and one of the area's best and state's oldest public libraries. After six months of searching, I found a rental dating from 1797 with wide front porch, gingerbread trim all about, uneven but gleaming wood floor boards, and big windows that allowed in plenty of sunlight. The home was too expensive to rent, but I made a bid to buy, even though it wasn't on the market. I had a tiny gut worry that it might cost me a lot in maintenance due to its age. I was assured by a contractor before the purchase that it was in good shape and most of the big work had been done. The reality is another story, book, or HGTV reality show about why you shouldn't believe everything a contractor says. Some are eager to get a naïve female buyer as a client; others simply have different views of what expensive and affordable mean.

Back to the house. The sellers and I negotiated and soon had a deal. Then, panic set in. How could I move a thousand miles away and buy a house on my own without my family checking it out? How could I manage all the costs on my own? I felt like the first-time homeowners I wrote advice for in many of my real-estate-focused articles and books with Margaret: Don't take on too much expense with the initial purchase. Be sure you can handle all the related costs and repairs, have an emergency fund covering at least six months in case disasters strike or you lose your income. Have a big, eat-in kitchen since that's where people gather today (it didn't). Have an even bigger deck since everyone wants to be outdoors (it didn't have that either).

At the same time, I also knew I was now part of the largest cohort buying a home: single women. And more important, I had become a member of the group who understood the psychic significance of having roots and the financial importance of not throwing money overboard each month on rent. This was an investment. I had to live somewhere, and this would eliminate flying back east, especially as my mother aged more, or being in an expensive shoebox in Manhattan. Moreover, I could go somewhere new because I had mastered how to lay the groundwork in a new location after three prior big moves.

I went online and found a local gym that charged an affordable twenty-five dollars a month. I searched and found a Pilates studio, as well as a painting class for if I had free time. I looked for a temple even though I wasn't particularly religious, but knew it would be a good place to meet others and secured names of two places to consider. I had already found a great grocery store that was stocked with inventory as appealing as Whole Foods, but far less costly.

Most of my friends thought I was insane, but after Chelsea Clinton became engaged and married in my village, everyone's reactions took a 180-degree turn. "How did you know to go there?" most asked incredulously. I didn't. And when my mother and daughters saw the house the first time, they were thrilled as they quickly each claimed a place to sleep. This would be our family's country home, too, even if we had to squeeze in. We would be together again at times.

After I moved in on the hottest day of the summer and unpacked eighty-two boxes with help from a high school friend, I developed a routine. I walked into town each morning to purchase the *New York Times* rather than have it delivered (it was good for exercise and human contact); I occasionally grabbed coffee at the town's version of the *Friends* TV show's Central Perk, where I became pals with the sales staff and recognized the retired folks who came to catch up; bought wine at a darling shop from an owner who cycled to work and left his shop door ajar daily when he'd take a quick coffee break or at least waved to that owner as I passed by. And I attended movies at a tiny theater where the prices then were a bargain $5 for a ticket and $1.50 for popcorn with real butter.

I fell in love with my new town and routine, but desperately needed friends. A visit to the town's most charming gift shop resolved that. The two perky, stylish, smart female owners, both from the Midwest, hugged me after we met and heard my saga; each had also been divorced and had children my kids' ages. They said they knew we'd become good friends. We have. A friend from the Midwest introduced me to friends in a neighboring town. I now had four friends and felt on my way. Someone might care if I didn't get up in the morning. The high school friend who had helped me unpack made it her mission also to help me acclimate and find more contacts. She came to visit regularly and took me by the hand into many other shops, explaining: "Barbara's new in town. You'll love getting to know her. She's a writer and also a good cook."

I found ways to enjoy my alone time, too. I planted my first-ever vegetable garden. Nothing made me happier each morning than going to check it out with coffee cup in hand to see what was ready to pick and use in cooking. I made gazpacho, spaghetti sauce, pesto, and fruit compotes from the fruits of my planting. I even learned to ignore a bunny that seemed determined to share in the spoils, and then came a deer . . . and another, despite a surrounding fence. I had become a country girl, much to the surprise of friends who considered me an urban sophisticate. So many friends came to stay from various parts of the country that I sometimes felt I was running a bed and breakfast. I also felt vindicated by my choice of a home when the locals I met told me I had made a smart investment. When new acquaintances asked where I lived, they put extra stock in my living in the village versus the countryside. Who knew? Certainly, not me.

Also moving after a difficult divorce was my friend Susan B. Born and raised in the northern suburbs of Chicago, she went to college and graduate school outside the city and lived downtown only briefly before marrying the first time. She and her first husband moved back to the suburb where he had grown up and started to raise their two children. She also began building her successful interior design business there. And then he died suddenly of cancer. She continued to live in their home as an anchor for their young children. After three years of being single, friends introduced her to her second husband. She divorced him after seven years when she knew he had lied about almost everything in his life except his name and his graduate degree—his job, his finances, his prior life with his former wife.

Once he was out of the picture, she stayed put for a few years and then downsized to a smaller house in the area since her daughter was still at home; her son had gone off to college. "The kids had been through so much so I didn't want to change our location dramatically and head back to the city . . . yet," she says. To test the waters, she bought a pied-a-terre in Chicago and traveled back and forth for work, trying to add clients in the city. "I needed to learn to navigate life again there—how I spent my time, where I spent my money, meeting new friends. The world was so different there," she says.

Then, it was her kids who pushed her to relocate. "They told me to make the move, that I was ready." Two years after considering the idea, she sold their home and bought a bigger place in the city where she could set aside some space for her design work. She now goes back and forth with her design team still based in the suburbs and handling more work without her present all the time, which has been good for the team of five. And also good for her. "It's made me less frantic," she says. She has recognized that change doesn't need to happen at once or in a linear pattern. She's aware of the downside of what can occur. "What's the worst that might happen? I'd make another change again if I needed to, but nothing would be catastrophic," she says.

Moving Beyond

Five-plus years after moving in, I have newfound wisdom: an old house even in good condition demands too many constant repairs for my budget. Aging wood needs replacement, more insulation needs to be installed, trees grow—and not just in Brooklyn—and limbs must be pruned. In addition, steep stairs won't suit me in another decade. The sight of my oil company truck pulling up to fill the home's tank churns my stomach in a Pavlovian response. My young grandson lives too far even with the benefits of FaceTime and Skype and in-person visits every three to four weeks or so. I may not have found the perfect home, but I know that I have found the perfect type of community. It has embraced me as if I were a native.

And in the process I've learned the real secrets of buying a house on your own:

- Don't buy for anyone else but you. This is your house and don't think about how much space you need for family or even your closest friends' circle. They probably won't come as often as they say or hope, or you hope. You can always put them up at a local hotel, inn, B&B, Airbnb, or VRBO rental, or give them a list of places from which to choose.
- Understand all costs in addition to the purchase. There's a mortgage, real estate and school taxes, insurance, sometimes neighbor-

hood association costs or condo fees, trash pickup, water bills, lawn care and snow removal, electricity and oil or gas prices, needed repairs, and so on. I wrote all the time about such topics, particularly for first-time homeowners, which I felt like since I was doing this solo. It still seems overwhelming at times.

- Think long and hard about maintenance. These costs—and time—also add up rapidly, from heating to electrical expenses, cleaning, mowing, raking leaves, trimming and pruning, snow plowing, ice dam repairs, gutter cleanings, tree trimming, and more—particularly if you have a pool, which I don't. Are you ready to give up some personal pleasures—hair coloring, new outfits, travel, eating out—to support your new home? Be sure. I thought I was, but no longer regarding the travel—and hair.

- Know how hard it is to find good workmen. Be sure there are good local contractors and remodelers available and that you have the time and emotional stamina to take on big jobs at this stage— and alone. Beware the contractor who says, when asked about an estimate, "Oh, it won't be that much." You reply, "How much?" He or she says, "Don't worry." And, of course, you do, particularly after the first surprise bill. Time to move on to another contractor, and always get firm estimates in writing. If the contractor, who might be a really nice person, professes to know how to do all that you ask, go see examples of prior work and get references.

- Think about how you envision your home within a few years. If you feel you're going to have to redo the kitchen, bathrooms, paint, and add built-in bookcases, closet systems, new roof, central air, and new window treatments, budget for all with your purchase price, so you're not stretched—a terrible feeling particularly at an older age and often on a fixed income. I know. After remodeling three kitchens, making do now with old wood cabinets and granite countertops I dislike is fine. Instead, I changed the door knobs, added new lighting, and painted, ignoring those stories about how much a kitchen will help sell a home. Remodeling doesn't help your currently squeezed bank account. One area real estate salesman, in fact, said, "Don't do it unless you'll stay 10 years." And I certainly don't know my timetable.

- How much do you plan to get away? If often, do you feel comfortable leaving your house in the dead of a brutally cold winter or blistering hot summer when a storm may knock out power? You may need to hire someone to check on it or house sit, and that's extra dollars.

- How much do you want friends and family to visit? Some home-owners love a constant onslaught of guests, and making meals, stocking the fridge and wine cabinet, changing sheets, and show-ing guests their neighborhood. They're the 2.0 version of Bob Newhart who ran an inn on a TV sitcom. Others find it wearisome and start learning to say, "I'm busy; maybe another time." Set boundaries.

- Might you consider renting it out? Do you really want strangers sitting on your sofas, sleeping in your beds, using your coffee maker and spices, and checking out your photos and medicine cabinets? They will at some point. Extra income is nice but there are risks. The sharing economy provides good grist for the horror story mill, according to one 2015 news story (Bowman 2015). Renting these days may seem so personal, yet it's still a business transaction. So much can go wrong in a peer-to-peer contract. In a darker twist on the Airbnb experience, the host died while the guest was staying in her apartment. Jordan Ruttenberg's story came from an NPR broadcast by Mickey Capper.

> Ruttenberg, a student at Wesleyan University, relocated to Brooklyn for a summer job with his friend Connor. They booked a place through Airbnb. His host, whom they met once via Skype, was in California at the time. Midstay, Connor no-ticed messages on their host's Facebook wall in the tone of: "You have to pull out of this" or "We need you."
>
> After reaching out to a friend of the host, [Ruttenberg] learned she had overdosed and been pulled off life support. His arrangement turned eerie, as he continued to stay in this woman's apartment, with all her personal belongings and photographs.
>
> Ultimately, the host's brother contacted Ruttenberg, asking when his checkout date was, assuming the procedural manner of a business arrangement.
>
> "I recognize the tragedy in it," Ruttenberg says, "but our relationship with her was a logistical one. And so, her death for us was largely of a logistical nature."

Ruttenberg says he would still use Airbnb for short-term stays. (Bowman 2015)

- Ask your home insurance agent if you have adequate coverage. You need it for all your belongings and liability in worst-case scenarios, and especially if you rent out your home.
- Remember that nothing has to be forever. Going smaller, sparer, and greener, and to a prefabricated house or condo on one level and closer to my grandchild, sound divine to me at this moment in time. Less than 1,000 square feet with an open-style, living-dining-kitchen room would be the clincher. Yes, I've become another boring baby boomer eager to downsize. It's almost time.

REFERENCE

Bowman, Emma. 2015. "When the Sharing Economy Brings Unexpected Experience." NPR, April 27.

9

SUDDENLY SINGLE

MARGARET

BUILDING A NEW LIFE

My house and much of its contents were sold, a tangible sign that I was moving on. Emotionally, however, a big part of me still wanted to "go home"—a metaphor for reclaiming the life I had lost. I knew I couldn't go back. The house sale was a done deal, but when this task was complete, I was aware then more than ever that the bricks and mortar and possessions within that had meant so much to us as a couple, and that what I had shed was just stuff. Without Nolan, most of those things no longer mattered, and only heightened the loss.

Rebuilding and filling my internal well was something I had to focus on now. I was on my own for the first time and possibly forever. This hit me hard and probably after I had given away most of my husband's clothing and possessions. I needed to craft a new life, as a single person, that was meaningful for the rest of my life. Shedding the old way of life and many of the possessions was tangible proof that it was out with the old and in with the new. I was moving on.

Initially, the prospect terrified me. And even four years after my husband died, being alone, sometimes still does. The pain doesn't hit me as often, but comes in waves, typically around annual milestones—

birthdays, anniversaries, holidays, and celebrations of all kinds—when I realize my husband is not by my side.

At first, I treaded gently as I feared going forward. Accepting that singlehood could provide joy took time. Barbara sweetly warned me what the future might portend: "You're no longer part of a couple. Be prepared. You'll be courted initially, then start to be left out of social situations. This is a couples' town." It was her way of telling me not to take it personally. That's just the way it is. It was also her way of nudging me forward to begin to enjoy life on my own.

She knew what she was talking about.

That first year after my husband's death was a social honeymoon. I was feted day and night. Friends rallied. Family circled the wagons. When I'd run into couples I knew, they invariably said: "Hey, I need to call you. We want to take you for dinner." And frequently (but not always) I'd get a phone call and an invitation. I was an oddity, the first in my social circle to have lost a spouse. People wanted to be there for me.

These were temporary crutches. They got me through the fog—the first 12 months of grief. The reality of year two hit me like Hurricane Sandy. My former social life started to disappear like water finally receding after a storm. One weekend invitation after another evaporated as I found myself less often the third or fifth wheel at the dinner table, in conversations, sharing drinks, or attending concerts.

Was I now considered a social pariah? Were female friends nervous I'd steal their husbands? Where did I fit in? All those I knew as couples were living their meaningful lives. They were into their routines. Decent folks. Well meaning. Getting up, going to work, working out, eating, chatting, going out together. "Look at me," I wanted to scream. "My life has been derailed. What am I supposed to do?" The reality was it was up to me to figure it out.

To cope, I slowly began entertaining at home. Inviting couples to spend time with me by opening bottles of good wine, sharing hors d'oeuvres, and meals I'd prepare with great relish. Or, I would take couples out to restaurants to pay them back for taking me out. But the reality—I was still the third or fifth wheel who was reminded frequently of my status when asked, "How are you doing on your own? It must be hard. Are you going to stay in your home? Are you dating? What do you do on weekends, especially Saturday nights? Do you hang out with other single women?" It was as if all single women—widowed, divorced, or never married—were part of some special social cult. "Stick with your own kind," they seemed to imply.

At the same time, I was being hit from all sides with advice for my new single status: Find a project; go to classes where you'll meet people (translation men). Learn to speak French (mostly women). Take jewelry making or pottery (definitely women), or wine courses (men and a few women). Work out in a gym. Travel. Try yoga or Pilates. You'll love photography; buy a digital camera; learn Photoshop. Think positive. Be upbeat. Try Internet dating. I couldn't fathom the idea of dating via online or fix ups. I didn't want to date, kiss, or become intimate with a stranger. I simply wanted to start a relationship that would mirror where I left off in my marriage—that safe place that comes after years of living together and being part of a comfortable couple.

Yet, I found myself trying various tactics to see if I was still attractive to the opposite sex. I started wearing tight-fitting jeans and shorter skirts and using magic creams purchased by my mother that were advertised on TV by Cindy Crawford to erase wrinkles. I spent more time than ever primping in front of the mirror before leaving the house, to which my daughter said one evening, "Since when did you become so vain?" I replied, "Since I became a single woman."

I was still invited to some weddings, Bar Mitzvahs, and parties—but solo. I'd find each time once the music started, the couples at my table would get up to dance, and I'd be left alone. I'd head to the powder room to find refuge or leave the event early to avoid embarrassment. I'd go to movies at off times—never a Saturday night—so I wouldn't see anyone I knew who would feel sorry for me sitting there with only my jumbo bag of buttered popcorn.

In fact, going alone anywhere meant rejiggering my thinking. Grocery shopping for one who didn't want to cook for one meant I became a daily shopper of prepared foods for one, which I'd eat alone just for the sake of eating. "Oy veh," I'd moan while chomping on my oven-baked chicken breast from the supermarket. I greatly missed the daily companionship of a spouse, so I'd turn on TV news and carry on a monologue with the newscaster giving my opinion on cutting state funds for Medicaid or the latest approach to peace negotiations in the Middle East.

Like most successful marriages, mine had been built on consistency. For forty-two years, we projected a vision of oneness and solidarity.

Invite the Cranes, a fun and interesting couple who could mingle with all types and ages, a great package deal. We spent time with couples sipping wine in new area restaurants or trying the latest recipes in touted cookbooks at friends' dinner parties. We talked about our kids, jobs, trips. Nolan also knew about wine and music. I could engage anyone in conversation as I became known as the great interrogator.

Suddenly, I was only part of the package—the unwrapped, discarded part. I found myself sitting alone many Saturday nights tuning into to my son's live symphony broadcasts on the local NPR station, listening to my musician son's music on the Internet, or watching old movies on TCM and fantasizing about what it would be like to be Kitty Foyle aka Ginger Rogers, a single working woman who serendipitously meets a doctor who madly falls for her, or Betty Davis in *The Big Lie* who by default gets the gorgeous Yale-educated pilot.

Singlehood, once I got over the initial grief, had its advantages. It could be empowering. I could eat that piece of chocolate cake before dinner without anyone commenting. I could sit up all night reading with the light on, eat in bed, write at 3 a.m. without disturbing anyone. And then I finally heard the click: It was time for ME at last. And I liked the idea almost as much as the fabulous trips to Africa, India, and the Far East I fantasized about taking if I should come into some unexpected huge inheritance from a distant relative.

Yes, I was on my own, but once I accepted that reality, the worries were slowly dispelled. "I am single. I am a widow." I could say it and fill it out on forms and no longer feel self-conscious. I am fine. I'll get better once I rock it, and rock it I did.

In my grief support group, I met other women who were in the same situation as I was. We'd often show up with our faces drawn and eyes swollen from another sleepless night agonizing over loss. These women got me through the stages of widowhood—something we shared. We were a sisterhood. There were Joan, Pat, and Lauren, kind and lovely down-to-earth special ed teachers; gorgeous red-headed and flamboyant Robin who would entertain us with her colorful stories; Natalie, the tall and long-legged youngster of the group who resembled a Keane painting with her dark hair and dark doe shaped eyes; Rita, a classy well-heeled financial whiz who took several months to spill her guts to the group. I made several new, close friends this way.

I enlarged my world in other ways, too. I began to volunteer to tutor kids and met other wonderful new people when I took the necessary training. I became more proactive about meeting new people when I moved into my condo. I made concerted efforts to reach out to my new neighbors, inviting them over, sending notes when there was a death in their families or a happy occasion like the birth of a grandchild. I reached out as a single, and it was reciprocated as I was invited to dinners and outings, not part of a package deal. I even went on a first trip to visit my two sisters and youngest son in New York City, and navigated buying the ticket online, getting to the airport, checking my bags so I wouldn't have to rely on some man to help me hoist my suitcase into the upper bin, waiting in line to get through security after stripping off my boots and belt, landing and finding my suitcase, and picking transportation to the Upper West Side where both sisters live.

In making peace with my new status—not relishing it more, but accepting it—I realized I had exchanged one way of life for another, and in so doing had even broadened it. At last I could live with that.

When feeling left out because I was not invited to a dinner party or special event I heard about through friends, sometimes the sanest thing I could do was to walk away mentally. I began to accept that one party was just one party. There would always be others with new people, new conversations about a host of new topics, and new places to explore.

Along the way, I devised all sorts of strategies to cope with my singleness. And I began sharing them with friends and my grief support members who found themselves in the same situation and asked for advice:

- Learn to be alone. According to many trained health care professionals, before you can be really healthy and maybe part of a couple, you have to like being on your own. Rediscover what you liked doing alone and didn't, or find new activities to occupy just you—maybe watching all the classic movies you never did, rereading your favorite high school or college books, taking up knitting . . . whatever. The ultimate test: Stay home on a Saturday night and find ways to enjoy it.
- Stay busy. If you're working, continue doing so. It's a familiar routine with people you know. It also keeps your mind occupied. The tough part is going home to an empty, dark house.

- Make plans with friends for dinner or to have a glass of wine after work, so you first do something fun before going to that very quiet house. Sign up for classes at night like Zumba or a new foreign language. It's also a good way to meet new people.
- Develop a weekend repertoire. Weekends were toughest since I wasn't at work and seeing lots of people and wasn't always included at social events. I made sure to have plans at least one weekend night. On Saturdays, I started doing errands. On Sundays, I began visiting my mother in an extended-care facility to go through her mail, pay bills, and eat dinner with her while showing her photos on my phone or sharing stories about my work and kids. Sunday nights after dinner I reserved for watching *Downton Abbey*, *Wolf Hall*, or other favorite PBS programs.
- If affordable, start traveling. It's tough doing so alone, but visiting your kids if they live in different cities is good for you and for them. There are many more organizations sponsoring solo trips—for both genders, for just females, for LGBTs, and by interests (such as a jazz cruise). When you go, be friendly with your seatmate on the plane or train, or your tablemates on a cruise, again another way to connect with people, even if temporary. Meet people in your hotel by striking up a conversation either in the dining room, bar, or in the lobby. Who knows where any of this may lead? Barbara's widowed cousin by marriage met her second husband at a hotel bar in Malaysia. She told him she wasn't interested in romance, just good conversation over dinner. Romance and years of happiness have followed!
- Get a pet. A dog or low-maintenance cat can provide wonderful company, and it's someone who is happy to see you when you walk through the door. It's also a warm body in bed. Walking a dog keeps you in shape and is a great way to meet other dog owners. Also, join a dog park. This can become another new social circle. Having lost several animals to death, I wasn't ready, but it was on my radar as a possibility.
- It takes time, but adapt slowly to your new status and life. You can't go back. Make adjustments in your old habits whether shopping, eating, or just spending time alone. You are your own best friend. Take the time to relax, listen to the music you enjoy, watch the soap opera your spouse wouldn't watch with you. When eating

out alone, don't do it on a Saturday night if it makes you feel uncomfortable. Eat at the bar or counter. It's less lonely when you can banter with the bartender or waiter or even those sitting around you. Select restaurants known for lively, crowded bars. Some even have long tables meant for family-style meals and family or can just mean lots of folks in the same situation.

- Join groups to meet people. Go to wine tastings, your church or temple, a college alumnae association, a cooking class sponsored by a store like Sur la table or Williams-Sonoma, a library-based free book club. There are all kinds of places where other women and men of like interests gather.

- Volunteer. Nothing makes you feel better than doing something nice for someone less fortunate, and many have much sadder tales to share. Barbara started baking weekly for a Girls' Club, made friends of all ages, and picked up some terrific brownie and cookie recipes and techniques. Others find cooking at a soup kitchen rewarding, and at times other than Thanksgiving and Christmas. The bottom line is to meet other volunteers and help others feel good.

- Be seen. No one is going to knock on your door while you sit inside and brood. Michael Anthony, the main character on the 1950s TV series *The Millionaire*, wasn't real. Others also won't show up unexpectedly, but you can find them. It just takes time, sometimes lots of time, and interest.

10

BUT WHO'S COUNTING?

BARBARA

350, REALLY?

After not dating for thirty-plus years, I became a kid in a candy store when looking for a new man to replace the one who left me. I was terrified of being alone and became determined to find someone. Fast. Singlehood wasn't a status I was comfortable with, having bought into my parents' bookend ideals of marriage and a BA. I desperately wanted to love and to be loved again.

Not only had it been since Nixon was president that I had had my last date with a man who wasn't my husband, but never before had my self-confidence been so in the gutter. Suddenly single in my fifties, I needed validation from others, and not friends and family, that I wasn't a loser who bought into all the acrimony toward the end of my marriage.

I had no time to waste to restore self-esteem before folks might write my epithet: She died single, alone, lonely, and dumped. In the meantime, my dearth of self-confidence led to myriad questions: Could I still feel alive again? Would I every feel sexy again? Should I color my hair? Lose weight? Could I attract a man? What would I do if someone asked me out on a date? Who would pay? What were the customs these days? Where and how would I find someone? Were there any good men left? What would I do if I actually found one?

I initially asked friends, acquaintances, and even neighbors I barely knew if they knew of someone appropriate for me. Nobody did. A lot of people suggested I look up old high school or college boyfriends, but all the boys—now men—I knew from back then were happily married and thriving, or so I thought. I worked from home. So I was left to figure it out on my own. In fact, I had no idea where to find a man. eBay and Craigslist didn't seem realistic places to get what I needed.

I wasn't the bar-hopping type, even when I had been younger. Standing around a lounge sipping a whatevertini with house music thumping in the background and hoping for a smart man and potential new husband to catch my eye in the midst of a hungry crowd held absolutely no appeal for me. Nor did scoping out guys at the grocery store.

The truth was that I had absolutely no idea how to go about dating, which isn't easy under the best circumstances—like when you're young, beautiful, full of hope, and naïve. And it doesn't get any easier when you're AARP eligible, seasoned, wrinkled, sagging, and realistic about love, life, and baggage.

Fortunately, timing was everything, as it turned out. Between 1970 when I met my husband and the year 2000 when we separated, Internet dating had emerged and was spreading. Internet dating makes meeting men—of all kinds, with their varied backgrounds, interests, hairlines, waistlines, locations, happy and dysfunctional families—much easier, but finding Mr. Right can still be a huge challenge.

When I first went online after a cousin by marriage suggested it was the best way to find romance, and which she had done, I quickly became hooked. The Internet was home to a virtual smorgasbord of men to pick from—seemingly successful, well-balanced, loving, good-looking with fabulous families, and male toys (boats, sports cars, even airplanes), and optimistic outlooks . . . as well as those with some serious emotional challenges from old, unresolved issues and hurts, and trunks of scarring memories from horrible childhoods, bad marriages, worse divorces, and unbalanced needy kids. Internet dating, I soon realized, required doing one's due diligence as in a good business transaction.

In addition to being selective, I felt I had to be careful about where the men I dated lived. I resided in a midwestern city at the time, and, because social circles there tended to be small and its gossip grapevine fast and furious, I decided to explore possibilities in other cities where I could be anonymous, yet where I knew people who might vet potential dates. I decided initially to stick to the midwestern roots I had come to love and where I found the men to be smart and less pretentious than many I knew back east.

I first looked at possibilities in one midwestern city where I had cousins. An intriguing photo and profile popped up. Rob seemed tall enough, still had hair, and was wearing a tuxedo that connoted a certain cachet; was a widower after a long marriage and a lawyer with his own practice; and had two grown children. Perfect, I thought. Widowers hate to be alone. He might not be looking for permanent love, but definitely would appreciate a home-cooked meal. Having children had probably made him flexible, and they were about my girls' ages and might become friends. We would be the contemporary version of TV's *The Brady Bunch*. I had to nab him before any of the casserole ladies who circle widowers like vultures might. I was advised there's a small one-year window.

I e-mailed Rob with my profile name and he promptly wrote back. He insisted on knowing my real name, which I shared reluctantly. There had been something comforting about the anonymity the Internet provides, but I could understand why Rob would want to know my real name and how knowing it might be useful in, say, everyday conversation. So, I gave him my name and sent along a professionally shot, black-and-white photo that I had taken just for this purpose. People often refer to these as "glamour shots," and I suppose "glamorous" wasn't too much of a stretch. I looked pretty damn good in that picture, but that didn't mean I liked sitting for the portrait. I was embarrassed that I had to resort to online dating rather than have a high-school honey to rediscover, so I told the photographer the picture was for a book jacket. It wasn't exactly a lie. I might use it for that very purpose. Someday.

Rob and I soon were e-mailing regularly, then talking live 24/7, which cut into my work and sleep routine. Not that I minded. His sense of humor, which was another huge plus for him, quickly emerged in his e-mails. I desperately needed to laugh—and I was ready for some positive hilarity in my life. Rob was hilarious, the kind of funny that literally made me pee in my pants. My writing career seemed to intrigue him, along with my Steinway and piano-playing chops, which I dropped subtly into conversation when he said he played by ear.

I was on a high I hadn't felt in years. We wrote cute poems to one another, and I sent off a care package of name-brand foods—Jiffy crunchy peanut butter, Bumble Bee tuna, homemade chocolate chip cookies with lots of Ghirardelli chips and the best Virginia pecans—since he frugally bought only generic brands. I felt like a teenager as I printed out Rob's photos and showed them to any friends and family who would look at them. I gushed to anyone who would listen (and not raise their eyebrows) when I shared that Rob and I probably would marry as soon as my divorce came through.

There was one minor glitch: We hadn't yet met. No matter. I still knew he was the one.

Almost a year after our initial conversation, we planned my first visit. I would fly to his city. He offered to pay for my ticket, but I declined because I didn't want to feel obligated in any way. I'd stay at his house but in a separate bedroom. He would show me his city, we'd dine at his club, and if he turned out to be the Jewish version of Ted Bundy, I had a carefully crafted escape plan with my cousins and close friends. Each was assigned an appointed hour to call my cell and check throughout the weekend to see if I were still alive and well.

Margaret helped me pick out my wardrobe, and she drove me to the airport for my outbound flight. A couple hours later, I deplaned, wound my way through security, and I finally met Rob face-to-face. I'm sure my expression said it all, and not in a good way. Rob was much shorter than I expected and wasn't wearing that debonair tux.

I admonished myself for being superficial. With his wonderful sense of humor, we had a ball that weekend . . . until he drove me past the cemetery where his late wife was buried. Oddly enough, that killed some of the chemistry for me. By the time we were at the airport waiting for my return flight, I knew our relationship was over. And I think it was mutual.

It's no fun to experience the end of a romance, but I culled valuable lessons from my brief "relationship" with Rob:

- Don't wait so long to meet an Internet date in person. Expectations and fantasies build up and become huge—and probably impossible to meet.

- Widowers present their own set of peccadilloes—namely, putting a late wife on a pedestal. It's hard to compete with a dead woman. You'll never make brownies as well, fight as fairly, or kiss as smashingly.
- Intelligence comes from within rather than the pedigree of a college or grad school. Rob had gone to a college and law school I had never heard of, and yet he was among the smartest men I've ever met.
- Some men shade the truth —as do women. With men, it's often about height and financial status and, sometimes, how many times he's been married or divorced—or even if he's still married. Women tend to fib about weight and age.

So, what about Rob? All was not in vain. We remained friends for several years, checking in on each other every now and then. He continued to make me laugh, and he generously offered wise advice about legal matters regarding my divorce. It might not have been romance, but friendship at the time was just as important.

Not that I didn't still long for romance—and eventually sex. Almost as soon as the wheels on my return flight touched down, I was back online. I next found Alex from Washington, D.C., a city where I had friends and so it didn't feel completely alien to me. Alex would be the one. I was sure of it, and my friends were delighted at the idea of my relocating there—which, I knew, would happen sooner rather than later.

Alex was a businessman, and he had attended college with someone I knew. He loved to read, run, and cook, and he took me to the Smithsonian's National Zoo in D.C. when I visited him, which earned kudos for creativity. I also loved his Saab convertible, which seemed evidence to me of a pleasantly quirky personality. We had a nice weekend, but again there was no real connection. None of that hard-to-peg chemistry. And he had been married and divorced twice—then a deal breaker for me.

It was next onto Terry in Southern California. Fortunately, he lived close enough to the homes of two sets of friends in case of an emergency. He was a graduate of one of my daughters' colleges, which provided sort of a connection. And relatives shared a mutual friend in a neighboring suburb, so, at least metaphorically, he was almost the boy next door (even if he actually lived 2,000 miles away). He played Scrabble with an encyclopedic vocabulary and took me for long bicycle rides at which he was equally adept. His shopping routine, however, put the kibosh on a future together. He spent thirty minutes examining one salmon fillet at Trader Joe's for us to share. I feared I might starve with this guy if every dish on every plate for every meal took a half hour of consideration before purchasing a micro-sized portion.

As it happened, food would, indeed, be part of our downfall. After my second weekend visit, Terry hit me with a double whammy. He said he felt no chemistry, and he complained that the pound cakes I made were like bricks.

Insult my kissing, but never my baking. Game over. Next!

Having struck out in the Midwest and on both coasts, I was beginning to think geographic diversity was highly overrated. Even so, I decided to give one more area a try. I hadn't dated a Southerner yet and soon found one whose charming politeness and gray hair grabbed my attention every time I signed on.

Tom came at just the right time, right when my divorce was heating up. I was terrified and needed comforting, though I realized years later I hadn't really been ready for a full-on romantic entanglement. I had gone through some of the early stages of grieving a loss—shock, sadness, and worry—but not enough of the depression, and anger was just beginning. Later would come acceptance and, much later, joy at the absence of acrimony. Through no fault of Tom's own, my pent-up anger started to surface each morning when he called, saying in his very appealing slow Southern drawl, "Good morning, Babs," as he had nicknamed me. I shot back with, "Can you believe what's happened today?" He could, and didn't want to hear after a while.

Despite my failure at recovering as quickly as I had hoped, Tom and I lasted years as a couple and got to know each other's families and friends. Distance and differences, though, did not bode well. For starters, although we were both members of the Jewish tribe, our cultural differences and values were as wide apart as the Grand Canyon. I felt his city and region were still fighting the War of Northern Aggression—the Civil War. Our tastes were on opposite ends of the food spectrum, too, and he also liked to eat out while I preferred cooking and eating in. Other tastes varied as well. I was a technophobe; he was skilled, and kept telling me, "Learn to think like the computer does." How would I know that? He admired Bill O'Reilly, Sean Hannity, and Fox News while my leanings were New York liberal through and through. I was conservative, though, where he was not. Tom spent money too impulsively for my cautious ways. In the end, the gulf was too wide. I also felt he loved his dog more than me. And the tip-off in the end was the constant nit-picking about superficial stuff, such as my dressing too casually for a walk in his 'hood and not applying lipstick first, which really, I believe, were about his growing unhappiness with the relationship, as was I. We had reached the end and just weren't meant to be a forever. I was glad we hadn't rushed into a permanent commitment, and so was he.

Hanging out in the neighborhoods of these men was getting me down. A friend urged me to stop traveling to meet anybody and cut my losses sooner. I concurred, but quickly fell off the wagon when I took a train trip to Long Island when I was visiting my mother to meet a man who seemed interesting. Peter had just returned from Paris, and he also loved his dog (a lot, but not too much). I considered these positive signs. He promised to take me to a great restaurant in his area (a third gold star) and send me home via a car service (a fourth star, this one for generosity).

This was beginning to sound better and better. Peter earned a fifth star for valor when he told me he had been in a terrible accident in Paris while rushing to save a dog. But therein loomed a big question about his physical condition, and it didn't remain a question for long.

When I got off the train in Long Island, Peter could barely walk. We went to a bar and sat at the counter. Within minutes it was clear we had nothing in common, and the conversation never sparkled. I gulped down my food and said I wanted to leave, but I didn't escape before he invited me to a Super Bowl party. I politely declined, knowing this relationship had no future. A few months later, I read his obituary in the *New York Times*. The notice didn't list a cause of death.

It was time to date closer to home. Not that proximity guaranteed love. I next met a widower in my midwestern city who seemed to be looking to win the trifecta: wife, mother, and grandmother. I felt suffocated. I e-mailed him politely that we were done, and he retorted that he had met someone else anyway. I learned guys don't like to be rejected, either, even if they, too, know the relationship isn't right. I moved on.

As I visited New York and my aging mother more often, I focused on guys there and started to track numbers, names, and interests on an Excel spreadsheet so I wouldn't confuse one with the other. Seriously. I had to do this after one guy reprimanded me for mixing him up with another and accused me of dating too many men at the same time.

He was right. When I hit 250 dates, my friends were incredulous. How could there be so many guys available for someone of a certain age to date? There were, I assured them, as I signed up for more dating sites—match.com, rightstuffdating.com (for Ivy League grads), and eharmony.com, and this was before others surfaced such as OurTime, OkCupid, and Coffee Meets Bagel. In fact, there would have been even more if I hadn't narrowed the list according to some additional criteria I thought I couldn't live with.

Geographic Undesirability. After nixing plane, train, and long automobile trips, I caved for a guy in Connecticut only an hour and a half away. He promised me a lovely dinner if I came to him since he had a meeting to attend. By then I knew it was all about the conversation, connection, and chemistry, not a meal or a checklist. However, this particular guy pulled a bait and switch. Because of a torrential rainstorm, we stayed in, and I found myself juggling mediocre pizza on my lap while sitting on his couch and dodging his advances. At least he served great wine. I ate and drank quickly to get away as fast as I could. To add insult to injury, he didn't validate my parking ticket or pack up leftovers for the long drive back. I promised myself the next guy had to live closer.

Fully Cooked. At my age, I had to accept guys as they were. I couldn't expect them to change their ways, no matter how smitten with me they might be—or I with them. The frugal ones (read: cheapskates) who didn't tip 20 percent or never suggested food when we met for drinks at dinner time (are you reading this, Mr. Double-Degree-Harvard-College-and-Law?) probably wouldn't buy me fat pink peonies for Valentine's Day or even spring for supermarket carnations on my birthday. The sniffer who wanted to see if our tissue types were compatible seemed more quirky than rude, especially when compared to the one who asked about the square footage of my mother's New York City apartment and then inquired if I inherited it and whether I would have to share the proceeds. He also double dipped shrimp in a cocktail sauce, not a hanging offense but certainly unappetizing. Most troubling was the man who told me on our first date at the Metropolitan Museum of Art that he had a temper he worked hard to keep it in check, which he could do pretty well except when pushed. I agreed with everything he said and ran the other way as fast as I could.

Grammarian Masters. I admit it: My writing skills have made good grammar an imperative since my middle-school English teacher taught me to diagram sentences. I've never expected anyone else to do so (although I would have been highly impressed if they could have), but when so many guys confused "to" with "too," "your" with "you're," and "their" with "there," my antennae shot up—and so did the level of my disappointment. I gave many prospects a pass on "farther" versus "further," which took me some time to master, but I had to draw the line on those who didn't understand the difference between "it's" and "its." And when one guy e-mailed about getting together and closed with "C U later, K?" I knew he was trying too hard to be cool. I wanted someone less hip, even if I weren't necessarily looking for someone who could decipher Faulkner.

Age Appropriate. Friends urged me to experience a fling with a hot young hunk. A significant number of guys under age forty e-mailed me; maybe looking for their Mrs. Robinson for some quick rolls in the hay (they probably thought that any woman of my generation was desperate for sex). After several online conversations with a few of these bright young things, I knew I had to be able to talk about important milestones: Where were they when Kennedy died (President Kennedy, not JFK, Jr.)? Did his family build a bomb shelter during the Cuban Missile Crisis? This was much more relevant than how many guys the Kardashian sisters dated or wed. Of course, ageism went the other way, too. I found a seventy-something prospect for my mother online. (Why should she be alone?) After e-mailing him and raving about her and all they had in common—swimming and interest in current events, he told me she was too old, but that I would be perfect. "I just saw your profile, and you sound terrific and look adorable!" he wrote. "I would much rather meet you than your mother! No disrespect intended. Although I am seventy-seven chronologically, I doubt that you will find anyone my age who looks, acts, and feels more like sixty." I politely explained I was looking for a long-term relationship of decades.

Music to My Ears. It wasn't long before I realized that I found the sound of a man's voice to be important. It mattered if his voice conveyed confidence or sounded weak or annoying, or perhaps even sickeningly sweet in tone. I learned that I needed only one brief phone conversation to decide if I could listen to a lifetime of "Honey, please pass the Lipitor?" I also learned that I needed some to take a breath and stop talking. One very smart lawyer was fascinating to listen to about his famous cases on the first, then second, and even third date. After that I realized he hadn't asked one iota about me. When he commented, "You're such a good listener," I simply smiled and knew anything longer term wouldn't work.

Sense of Humor. I like bellyaching laughs. It took me time to realize that life with someone who was always serious could be deadly boring. I found myself never laughing at anything one regular date said. When he didn't get the humor in my suggestion that we had honed the art of bartering by trading his gardening for my cooking, he got competitive. He suggested his skills were "more intense" than mine. Granted, I had been cooking from the Food Network's easiest recipes, but I knew deep down that even Julia Child's duck à l'orange wouldn't cut it with his choice of Grey Poupon.

Clear Goals. I tried to be flexible and bend to someone else's attitude and way of doing things, but there were certain changes I knew I couldn't take. The twice-divorced guy who told me during our first phone conversation that he was never, ever going to marry again seemed a bad risk. Even if I wasn't sure I wanted to tie the knot again, either, I at least wanted to keep the option on the table. The very religious man who called multiple times also posed a problem. It wasn't the idea of no longer eating shellfish or a rare, juicy cheeseburger, but the fact that he always suggested meeting after sundown on a Saturday evening—sometimes 10 p.m. in the summer. Unlike my daughters who had similar late-night dating routines when they were younger, I usually tucked myself into bed by then.

Politically Correct. I once thought that voting along the same party lines was irrelevant. If Republican Mary Matalin and Democrat James Carville could find long-term joy together, so could I, a liberal Democrat. After dating a few conservative Republicans, especially during election years, and finding today's political climate increasingly vitriolic, I knew having a strange political bedfellow was a recipe for a bad night and worse day. Opposites don't always attract.

Character or Charisma. Even the most winning personalities—effusive salesmen types who perfected the art of flattery—became suspect when cracks in their character surfaced. After swooning over a guy with a megawatt–light bulb personality who was almost as funny as Rob, I gradually found he sucked the air from the room with his narcissistic need to exaggerate to make himself look better, seem more powerful when he was already successful, and gaslight or deny he did or said what he did, as I took a crash course in learning all I could about this type of personality. I finally heeded actress Laura Linney's wise words, which I had read in a magazine article about why she dumped a guy: "Charisma is not character." It took too long but we bid adieu, I breathed clean air again, and learned that character trumps all, from perfect incisors, to a full head of hair, to front row seats at a winning Broadway show.

There were so many others along the way who had to be eliminated for reasons that bothered me but wouldn't trouble others. (Although some might say I was excessively picky, I didn't want a second divorce.) A nice man who took me to one of New York's best French restaurants had to go in part because of a facial twitch I tried to ignore but couldn't, despite one daughter's urging me to be more empathetic. I was but . . . . More important, though, was that he terrified me after our second date when he told me he was going off the JDate site because he had met the woman of his dreams: me!

The guy who wore a gold chain and compounded the déclassé look by unbuttoning his shirt to show his hairy chest also had to go. So did the one with a Donald Trump-style comb-over and terrible, crooked, stained teeth. As did the smart, university-employed professor who wrote learnedly about wine, including how Château d'Yquem is too expensive to drink often, or that a JJ Prüm Wehlener Sonnenuhr Spätlese or Auslese is appropriate for wedding celebrations. I also had to nix the guy who shared over lattes and espresso in a small, charming Italian restaurant that he and his former wife loved to stay home on New Year's Eve to "do it all night." Before I escaped, he managed to say he had lost interest in me by the time we were served the veal Marsala.

Dating revealed as much to me about myself as it did about all those guys. I had evolved through the years and come to understand what it took for me to be happy and what wouldn't work for me. I could pretty much tell right away whether there was some of that elusive chemistry—a pitter-patter—when you see the same guy time after time. It was often a gut instinct rather than checking off characteristics on the mental list I had started with when dating—smarts, profession, graduate degree, humor, family, finances, and health. There was less need for a second or third date if my internal instinct sounded a strong no. I became the Queen of the First Date and sometimes Queen of the First Date-and-a-Half.

After getting over my skittishness about my post-divorce, romantic choices, I stopped asking family and friends what they thought of the guys I introduced them to, though many still offered their opinions. It took me a while to learn that what mattered wasn't whether others accepted him, but what I thought about him. And what he thought about me, which usually became crystal clear early on.

From that I learned another lesson that took time to accept. Not everyone found me provocative, attractive, desirable, smart, sexy, kind, and even funny. Guys turned me down for being too short, having dark rather than blonde hair, laughing too loudly, living too far away, too often mentioning my alma mater that I loved and where I did a lot of volunteering, not understanding football or March Madness, carrying too many pounds at times, being overly enthusiastic, not being the right religion or age, bringing up incidents from the past too much, and for reasons never shared (but which I'd love to know, or maybe not).

After my husband left me, my mother kept telling me that "good merchandise doesn't remain on the shelf." I tried to believe her, but it was hard not to lose faith after literally hundreds of dates. I was still looking for Mr. Right after my Excel spreadsheet had grown to too many pages with details from many of my 350 dates. I was buoyed, though, after I heard about a woman who met her prince after 413 dates. I had just 63 more to go!

The Dating Merry-Go-Round

In the three decades since I had last dated, so much had changed. Much of it for the better: Internet dating made it easy to avoid grungy bars and stale pick-up lines from shady guys. Of course, there was no guarantee that a winning Internet profile would immediately transport Mr. Right to the front door—I'm certainly proof of that—but I have learned a thing or two about making the most of this new technology.

First of all, how you market yourself is important. Think of yourself as the latest Internet invention, ready to be scooped up for billions of dollars by Google or Facebook—if you stand out as a winning prospect. Second, keep in mind that meeting a new man face-to-face, in an actual public place at first and not in some virtual setting and early on before fantasy takes hold is imperative. And then there are some other tips that can be useful:

Craft a stunning profile. Write a compelling but truthful profile. Be honest about your age, height, and weight. Have a friend proofread and critique it for you. It's hard to be objective about yourself, and having a trusted friend share her input is priceless. Also, use a really good photograph. It doesn't have to be professionally taken, but it needs to be a recent, close-up portrait taken within the past year or two. Offer a full body shot that's recent. This is crucially important to the men who are scoping you out online. In fact, one prospective date actually called me the morning of our dinner to ask how much I weighed since I had posted only a head shot. When I refused to disclose that information and offered to nix the evening, he relented (likely out of sheer embarrassment). Avoid posting photos featuring dogs or cats—it's a cliché that doesn't work, according to men I've interviewed. Finally, pick an interesting, provocative profile name.

Be honest about your location. Many men don't want to date anybody more than thirty to forty-five minutes away. I sometimes shaded the truth because I was willing to relocate for the right guy, since my career demanded only my laptop and a cell phone. But shading the truth sometimes backfired. One man was furious to learn that I was looking in Boston when I spent most of my time in New York, even though I said I had friends there and didn't find New York guys appealing. He said I had done this when I lived elsewhere and looked in New York. He remembered my storyline. Bottom line: He told me I was among the most dishonest people he had ever met (his actual diatribe was much longer and harsher and not worth repeating). I got defensive when I e-mailed him back. Several e-mails later we reached détente.

Share your real interests. So many women talk about loving sushi, being vegetarians, and enjoying long walks on the beach that they sound fungible. Find what makes you distinctive from the masses. What are your passions (and I don't mean this in a sexual way, though some men asked me that, too)? For me it was having someone to cook with or who loved food, travel, tennis, and dance, and who read books and the *New York Times*. I also wanted a TV companion who would watch some of the shows I adored, including *Downton Abbey* and *The Bachelor*. Be honest with yourself about what risks you're willing to take. If the thought of going up in a tiny plane gives you hives, don't expect some dashing guy with a pilot's license to land at your feet. My biggest half-truth was that "I gardened," after one date told me men love women who get down and dirty and I should add that to my profile. I think he had something else in mind.

Don't whine. If you hate your parents, siblings, former spouse, or current or former boss, you don't need to share that online or even on the first or second date. Being upbeat is important; perky, however, can be overkill.

Beware of stranger danger. It's a meat market out there, and sometimes vulnerable and desperate females can be duped by the guy who seems to be The One. You like his bio and the way his photos look, his voice is sexy, and he brags about his successful career, but not too much—just enough so you know he can pay for dinner. You're almost hooked. And then the scam. He gets you to trust him and hits you up for money. If your gut speaks to you at all, if it tells you even in the tiniest whisper that something's not right, trust it earlier rather than later.

Be gracious. Don't be a taker. Many men will pay for the first date—wine, coffee, lunch, even dinner—and they should. However, you should offer to split the meal, either the first time or on a subsequent date. Also, don't insult anybody online; it's not a good start. If you talk or meet and then find you have no interest, say so gently. One potential date and I agreed to be honest when we met at a restaurant. He looked me squarely in the eye and said, "So, what do you think?" I replied, "This won't work for me." He was glad I was honest, said "no hard feelings," and we parted right then and there. I felt bad, but a deal's a deal.

Don't burn bridges. The world is small—and getting smaller every day, which I found out the hard way when I learned that some of my Internet dates had heard about one another, even though they lived in distant cities. I discovered firsthand that "Midwestern Rob" was dating an old friend of Tom's, and that one New York City date had also dated Tom's honey. Have you kept this straight? Better to speak nicely of everyone than gossip. Remember, too, if someone's not interested in you, don't take it personally. As I found in one case, he may have met someone, but might not be ready to get off a site yet . They even might still be married or be too recently widowed. You could remind them too much of a former spouse they couldn't stand, or even their mother or former mother-in-law, or you simply might not meet their checklist of requirements or register high enough on their chemistry lustometer. I never knew that existed until one date told me that over lunch—in between bites—he wasn't feeling lust. Maybe, it was simply indigestion.

Along the way, I regained enough confidence to find that being single offered its own set of rewards. In fact, as I healed I found it wasn't as bad as I imagined it to be, once you no longer feel you're wearing a giant *D* for divorced or dumped on your chest, regain your sea legs to live, and accept that your new life will be good—maybe very good—just different. Some people even find they don't want to go back to a permanent partnership, though they may seek romance.

Here's what I found I loved about my new status:

- New me. I got back my maiden name, which required reapplying for it legally. I regained my sense of optimism and was grateful to be alive.
- New changes at home. I got to sleep in the middle of the bed, and hog all pillows and blankets. I didn't have to share closets. I didn't have to make the bed. I didn't have to put on a roll of toilet paper, but could set it on the back of the commode. I could eat dinner standing up in front of the TV in my kitchen. I could eat in bed watching TV when I wasn't standing in front of the kitchen TV. I could keep to one TV station rather than have programs interrupted and switched. I could watch sappy TV shows on the Hallmark or Lifetime channels. I could work any time of the day or night when creativity struck. I could grab whatever section of the newspaper I wanted first, especially the Sunday *New York Times* and its Style and Business sections. I could make a good cup of coffee with my new machine and milk frother, but first ask a guy to program it. Some habits don't die. Full disclosure: I never tried first reading the manual.
- New financial savvy. I could make smart financial choices for investments (with help from an advisor); buy my first car (but first

ask every guy I knew who loved cars what they thought of possible choices); find and buy my first house on my own; research and find good health insurance, home insurance, and long-term care insurance. I could entertain at home or at restaurants on my own, and select the wine, keep the conversation and wine flowing, signal the waiter to hand me the bill rather than a guy at the table, and calculate the tip. I could entertain because I liked people, rather than because it was good for business getting.

- New habits. I could send out holiday cards without being embarrassed that it was from me and not a traditional family of four. I could make contributions just with my name rather than "Mr. and Mrs." I could comfortably check the "single" box on forms and not feel I was the biggest loser in ways other than weight. I could spend time with relatives and pals without anybody's feeling neglected. I could think of myself in a way I believe, rather than buy into what I'd been told. I could be a good role model to daughters and show them that the world doesn't fall apart permanently when you don't have a partner in your life; that you can be happy and thrive, successful in all sorts of ways even if you weren't raised to think that way. I could stop reserving "I love you" just for a spouse, but tell it to my close friends and family at the end of many conversations.

- Out and about. I could be braver now about flying and do without my former rituals, except on the most turbulent flights—nothing compares to the fear of being dumped and left after 50. I could walk into events on my own, making conversation with strangers, and drive myself home at night. I could become comfortable as a third or fifth wheel with friend couples who valued my company. I could eat at a counter alone in a simple diner or fancy restaurant and schmooze with a waiter or bartender and not feel I had to explain why I was alone: "He's out of town." "He's sick." "He's sick of me!" I could attend reunions and feel OK (not great) that I didn't get to celebrate a 40th anniversary as some of my friends did and would be able to do.

- New future. I could look forward to meeting someone who would value me for who I am, love me unconditionally, and promise a forever. On the flip side, I would seek someone whom I value for who he is, love him unconditionally, want to be with him forever, and decide what to call him without consulting anyone. I would know that I'd be OK, even if I don't meet that forever someone. I know that I have the biggest vote—maybe the only one—in where I retire, when, if I can, and where I'll end up in perpetuity.

11

REMODELING YOURSELF

MARGARET

INSIDE OUT

PARIS—I step onto the runway. The crowd turns to stare in my direction. Anna Wintour, editor-in-chief of *Vogue* and the single most powerful fashion editor in the world, sits wearing her dark glasses that help convey her typical icy demeanor. Next to her is Grace Coddington, her lieutenant and creative director. No matter, across the room I spy Glenda Bailey of *Harper's Bazaar,* and oh, there's Alex White, known for resurrecting *W.*

Loud music blasts and lights flash. TV cameras follow my every twist and turn. People in the audience begin to tweet, post on Facebook and Instagram, shoot short videos. Flashbulbs pop. Getting snapped makes the whole scene feel like some endless Kardashian dream, though for me it's a bit of a nightmare. What would people back home say if they could see me now?

Over in the corner I spot Marc Jacobs, Donatella Versace, Zac Posen, and Oscar de la Renta, one of his last appearances before he died. Their eyes are glued on me. I am unfazed and hold my head high. I feel gorgeous and sexy, my almost-six-foot frame is trim and fit. I glide back and forth on the catwalk wearing a little black day dress by Alexander McQueen in crepe de Chine with crystal-flecked shoulders. My hair is teased and piled high on my head and Yeprem, eighteen-karat, white gold, diamond, climber earrings dangle.

I clutch my Judith Leiber pearl-encrusted bag; point my stunning, silver, Prada pumps with black grograin bows; and jiggle my Hermes, colorful, enamel, signature bracelets. Thunderous applause breaks out. I step down into the audience where Lester Holt is waiting to interview me.

After all, it's my show; and I'm a star!

"Meg, get up," my mother commands.

I am 12 years old. It's a lovely warm Saturday morning, and my mother wakes my sister and me to go shopping for spring clothes. What would be exciting for most preteens leaves me with a feeling of dread. I loathe this routine and grunt a few times while dragging my short chubby body out of bed. My stomach churns thinking about the dozens of outfits I'll have to try on that will only make me more self-conscious about my body that brims with rolls of baby fat as I listen to my mother, clicking her tongue in disappointment. And the comments: "Meg, think before you put that caramel or piece of chocolate cake in your mouth. If not, I'll have to start shopping for you in the chubby department."

From the word "go," my mother has endlessly told me I was too fat and too high waisted (not much I could do about that) to wear the clothes that are trendy. It's 1958—what could look worse on a short, chubby, undeveloped twelve-year-old than a full-circle skirt resembling the kind used to cover up a Christmas tree stand, or a pencil skirt that reveals every bulge and accentuates my high waist when worn with a tucked-in, crisp, white, cotton, man-tailored shirt.

My sister and I are always well dressed. My mother sees to it, requires it. Dressing properly is part of her fantasy of the perfect looking '50s family. Quite frankly, I always maintain a certain insouciance about my appearance, although I do care about my hair, which is a source of pride as it is long, dark, thick, and wavy.

This lack of concern about appearance follows me into adulthood. My mother-in-law hints, "Meg, let me take you shopping." I decline. My friends suggest that it might be nice if I'd go with them to look for a dress or blazer. I decline. Throughtout my forty-two-year-marriage, daily dress is for comfort—jeans, a work shirt or tee, and loafers or flats. I work from home and often go to my "office" in my PJs.

Since I have pierced ears, I wear earrings, but other than that, I lack interest in accessorizing with other jewelry, scarves, belts, fancy purses, designer shoes, even makeup, which is minimal and purchased at a nearby Walgreens. And if I have to dress up for a wedding or big party, I generally gravitate toward plain tailoring, neutral colors, lightly constructed dresses, slim-cut pants, and pullovers. My husband always thought I looked terrific and was great at complimenting me whatever I wore. He was the one with the fashion sense with his chic, tailored jackets, suits, and fabulous ties.

Jump ahead to age 64. I am suddenly single. At first, I am too sad to care about how I look. I am very thin, too thin, from the stress of losing my spouse and getting my house in shape to sell and, for once, I have little appetite. And then about a year after losing my husband, going to one-on-one therapy and a support group where I meet and socialize with new people, I am ready to go out into the world again, albeit a different world for me.

Fashion is the way we compose ourselves every day. For me it becomes an external sign that I am embarking on one of the biggest changes of my life in a positive way. Although I'm not consciously thinking about it, I start to pay attention to little things in my appearance—taking time to fix my hair before going downstairs to get the mail, dressing a little better and sexier for I never know who I'll see on the elevator or at the grocery store. I want to test the waters to see if I am still desirable and able to catch the eye of a man. It is as if I have pressed a button and poof, I had morphed into a full-fledged, vain person. My mother would be so proud.

I start wearing chic workout pants that my daughter sends me for my birthday. I begin shopping at Gap and Banana Republic stores to buy slim jeans and cropped pants with flattering tops in bright colors to set off my dark eyes and pale skin. For the first time, I do one of those non-surgical face masks that makes you look like a kabuki dancer. I buy moisturizers and Pro-retinol products by the caseload (still purchased at Walgreens). I channel Nora Ephron (it's all about the neck, as she writes) and Diane Keaton from the movie with Jack Nicholson, *Something's Gotta Give*, as I begin to toss aside my turtlenecks and shirts with mandarin collars for plunging Vs and spaghetti-thin T-straps. I purchase new shades, powders, and lipstick hues at Macy's. I walk by the perfume counter on my way out and give myself a few spritzes of those $100-plus, name-brand choices from Lancôme, Chanel, Prada. I invest in fancy and pricy haircare products on one hand to smooth the frizz, and on the other to add body to my naturally wavy hair.

What used to take me 20 minutes tops to do—get ready to go out— is stretched to an hour as I try on outfit after outfit, throwing what I don't like on the floor, hoping to find the most flattering one or sitting before the mirror preening and primping, tweezing my brows, and filing my nails. When my kids come for a visit, they roll their eyes when catching me peering into every mirror I pass. "Who are you, mom?" they jest.

But my makeover needs to be more than external. As we all know, beauty can be shallow and intellect can be challenging. But when they get together, they can be a powerful force. I can work on both. After boosting my appearance, it's time to improve the world and my mind. I take inventory of my skills and sign up for training to tutor elementary school kids in reading and writing.

At the same time, I broaden my mind with a steady diet of classical music, opera, theater, and art. I learn how to do Twitter, post on Facebook, use an iPhone, write and post information on a website, and edit photos. I take classes, including some fancy cooking courses just in case I meet the right fellow and want to impress him with my culinary skills. "Oh, this was nothing," I will say as I whip up a tangy, tomato-based, fish stew or prepare a savory, spicy gumbo, which have required hours of recipe finding, shopping, prepping, and preparing. I then work on my body. I shore it up with yoga (too slow) doing the upward and downward dog, or Pilates with a trainer (too strenuous) with its planks and Rolling Like a Ball exercises. I start taking daily walks as a great way to get out and meet people. Of course, I have to dress for that occasion, too. Oh, this is taking up just so much time and energy!

However, after reinventing myself, I am ready to make my grand entrance. The stage is set. I fantasize floating down a hallway to meet a man and wowing him with my dazzling figure, shoulder-length wavy hair, flattering clothes, and improved mind, while I tell him how I am volunteering to save the entire world, not just one tiny little section. I am interesting. "I am woman," sang Helen Reddy. I am the new best me.

This is what I do because I want to, and I finally reach a place where I can. No prompting. No pushing. For the first time ever, I feel I deserve it. I dare to love myself. By doing so, my life becomes a hit show with me as the star.

BARBARA

THE WEDDING DIET™

STOCKHOLM—I rarely compliment myself, but I look regal and svelte as I stride up to the podium in my white, sequined gown to accept the Nobel Prize in Economics. It's not every day that a sixty-something, Jewish gal from the 'burbs gets this award from the King of Sweden. And I'm not the least bit nervous after all the interviews I've done—a *Today Show* EXCLUSIVE! with Matt Lauer, not just Katie Couric, Meredith Vieira, or Savannah Guthrie; the cover of *People* magazine; a serious chat with *NBC Nightly News* host Brian Williams (before his steep fall from grace); and some girls' gossip with comedian Ellen DeGeneres, who thinks it's hysterical that someone without an economics PhD would snare this prize for discovering—are you ready—a global diet that's helping to eradicate world obesity affordably. And it wasn't even named after a town (Scarsdale) or area (South Beach).

My carefully tested The Wedding Diet made headlines after word spread that an aging mother dropped twenty-five pounds in twenty weeks to look good for her daughter's wedding, kept it off, and did so without surgery, an arsenal of drugs, a movie-star career turned toxic, or convoluted diet book instructions that are hard to remember. Mothers everywhere beg their kids to marry, whether they're the right age or in love. And you thought *Tiger Mother* was pushy?

I only wish my diet plan garnered such attention, but it worked for me. When my younger daughter announced her engagement after eight years of dating the same young man, it wasn't the logistics of planning a wedding for 150 that terrified me. I had fifteen months—an eternity for someone organized, who doesn't overanalyze the merits of asparagus spears wrapped in smoked salmon with caper garnish versus tuna tartare in phyllo with horseradish dabs. It's really NOT THAT HARD bridezilla moms! But losing twenty-five pounds—the size of a plump Thanksgiving turkey—and looking elegantly sexy is tough. My older daughter doesn't sugarcoat the urgency. "The photos last forever," she says.

I know this is my younger daughter's important day but, after my daughter and her husband, I feel like I am also in the spotlight in front of many people who haven't seen me in ages. I want to look gorgeous. I certainly don't want to be seen as a washed-up divorcee who let herself go. I must confess, there is a part of me that's thinking, "Let my ex eat his heart out. Look what he gave up even if he doesn't think so."

I hatch my plan. I rejoin Weight Watchers when I realize I weigh more than I did during my first pregnancy. I give up foods I love: butter, eggs, cheese, processed sugar, pasta, mayonnaise, red meat, French fries, cream soups, Bumble Bee tuna in oil with mayo, Russian dressing, bagels, risotto, gnocchi, Skippy chunky peanut butter (not the reduced fat variety), and almost anything white—rice, potatoes, bread. I eat healthier: oatmeal, lettuce, tomatoes, cucumbers, apples, sweet potatoes, mushrooms, onions, beets, avocados, chicken, salmon, and more chicken to the point where I'm almost clucking and growing feathers. I just can't bring myself to add tofu, despite everyone's raves that it can taste like anything you pair it with. I never like wannabes. As food guru and writer Mark Bittman says, why would you go for anything but the real stuff—that is, margarine versus BUTTER.

I crank up my exercise: a weekly Pilates class since everyone says it will reshape me; a weekly training class with a cute, toned trainer who I've told to be brutal. The other five days I do cardio on the treadmill or elliptical, plus 100 sit-ups, 100 jumping jacks, and at least five minutes of jumping rope. I'm obsessed—and exhausted. In my free time, I do my work to pay for the fitness and healthier foods.

The first three weeks are depressing. The scale doesn't budge. But I overcome the initial hurdle: I resist emotional binging. There's no turning back. In fact, I avoid almost everything bad. Lunch with a friend and his grandchildren at a pizza parlor on a cold, snowy day tests my mettle. For the kids and himself, he orders a large hot pizza dripping with mushrooms, pepperoni, gooey cheese, and fat garlic knots. Without knowing I'm dieting, he suggests I have the garden salad with cold chicken. Does he think I need to lose weight? Do I look that fat? I ogle his choices but dare not ask for a bite. Gradually, the digits move down. My old skinny wardrobe starts to fit. I get a bit cocky. Maybe, I can go for 30 pounds? Do a triathlon?

Back to reality. After I shed seventeen pounds—the size of a smaller Butterball turkey, I'm surprised not to get the responses I expect. A sales clerk at a favorite makeup store flatters me, "You've lost weight," then adds, "Your face looks much thinner." She thinks she's tossing me a compliment. Who cares if you've got a thinner face? To me that implies being gaunt, haggard, tired. My fuller face makes me look healthy; this suggests the opposite. I imagine my magic bullet wasn't exercise and dieting, but a rare, undiagnosed, terminal illness. If that's my fate, the silver lining is that I can eat piles of pasta with fresh mozzarella and Tuscan fries dipped in mayo. Fortunately, I know that's unlikely. My appetite is robust, and I've been to the doctor.

Hope finally rears its head. A friend who hasn't seen me for weeks feeds me the thin-face compliment, but adds another, "Your legs look thinner." I try to be gracious, even though my pants cover them up. Does she have X-ray vision?

I find myself working my weight loss into every conversation to force compliments; an easier alternative might be to wear a big sign. At my favorite bra store where the specialty is perfect fittings, I explain, "I need new bras because I've lost seventeen pounds." The saleslady replies matter-of-factly, "That's nice, dear." I'm disappointed, but then she's never seen me. When a server at a chic New York restaurant asks if I want bread, I give him a piece of my mind, "WHY would you ask?" I try to add sweetly, "I've just lost seventeen pounds."

When a nice young salesman at a department store finds dresses for me for the rehearsal dinner, I quizzically eye the tags and correct him without screaming—"HAVEN'T YOU NOTICED my thin face and legs?" Instead, I gently say, "I'm so sorry. I don't think you can tell with my coat on that these are too big. I've lost seventeen pounds."

The dresses look good, but aren't perfect. They're a bit snug in the abdomen. Yet, my older daughter's impressed, "WOW, they *almost* fit," she says with encouragement. I add a Pilates class. Yes, I've become obsessed.

Three months later and eight more pounds down, my wedding outfit—a chic black lace dress with delicate sleeves over a goldish beige background—fits perfectly. My new single-process, dyed, longer hair-style and new skin-care and makeup routines have taken years off as well. As I walk the bride down the aisle, along with my former husband, I feel triumphant. Two days later, I dig into my favorite thin-crust pizza and fries and tell those with me, "I'm not sharing." The best reward? I feel good about how I look with the new me! And I have learned that reality can be better than fantasy.

More Remodeling Tips

Divorce can cause your self-esteem to plummet. It's emotionally and physically devastating. Losing a spouse from death or divorce can cause complete inertia. However, we were determined this wasn't going to happen to either of us. To feel better and make ourselves more appealing to the opposite sex, Barbara went to work on herself, even before the wedding, as if she were a remodeling project. Margaret had a delayed reaction. She was grieving until she realized it was time to take control of her new life. It took two years to reach that point. It would begin with a makeover of body and mind. Both of us used all the knowledge we could glean from women's and lifestyle magazines and online, as well as what caring friends and, in Barbara's case, some super smart sales staff advised. None of the shared wisdom may sound terribly new, but it was the first time we put it all together to be the best looking, healthiest that we could be, given our ages, limited finances, and sadness about our circumstances.

It's all about the hair. Listen to your friends who have style. One highly confident friend with a great cut and color insisted Barbara visit her hair salon in New York City. The cost almost rivaled the national debt, but it was fabulous, and the staff served wine and lattes so she could forgo lunch. She had her local, less-expensive person take over with the color and only went back for cuts every three to four months. Later, at the suggestion of one hair stylist, she started adding highlights for some sparkle twice a year. Margaret colored her hair, a single process, but it was starting to look like a helmet. She asked her colorist to add some streaks and had her hair cut with multiple layers. None of this is cheap. However, if you were to take a poll, most women with limited funds would confess they'd give up Starbucks, wine, pedicures, magazine subscriptions, and maybe even men, but never their haircuts and color.

It's also about the skin. Barbara wasn't one to indulge in facials given the costs and she had inherited her nintey-something mom's almost wrinkleless face, but she still needed that occasional glow. She found a great esthetician and treats herself a few times a year to removing dead layers, which seems to rejuvenate the sometimes deader parts of her in the dead of winter. Margaret, who also has good skin, started using fancier moisturizers and masks her mother ordered through the Home Shopping Network, and she had her first facial, thanks to a gift.

Don't forget the color. Barbara tended to wear makeup rarely and only for important occasions and dates. She disliked spending the time primping. Her local makeup shop gave her a good lesson in a quick fix—moisturizing, foundation, the right colors, ways to accent her best feature—her large green eyes—and some eye liner and mascara. She kept her eldest daughter's suggestion for a daily regimen taped to her bathroom wall to be sure she'd moisturize and more. You don't have to help the aging genies was the gist of her daughter's sweet lecture. Margaret, who never wore foundation or lipstick, now wears tinted moisturizer and lip gloss. She also bought the kind of toothpaste that makes her teeth white. We're so vain.

Go for Michelle-style arms. Barbara had let her body go, too, so she combined Pilates with regular, gym, cardio workouts. She walked whenever she could and always took stairs rather than an elevator, parked far away in parking lots so she'd have to walk. She started bicycle riding around town on a new, shiny, red bike with a Toto-style basket, and imagined herself in France pedaling for a daily baguette. (Of course, with her regimen, it was a fantasy loaf since to consume it would have set her back.) She considered running a marathon with her kids and signed up, but chickened out. A half-marathon is still in the back of her mind to do before she dies or the knees give out. Altogether, she spent way more than she'd like to admit, but not only did the pounds and flab come off, her cholesterol and blood pressure went down dramatically, too. Margaret avoided exercise as much as possible and, since adulthood, has been slim. But osteoporosis runs in her family so she figured it was time to start moving and purchased a treadmill, which she uses at least five times a week for at least 30 minutes. This also keeps her figure in check as she huffs and puffs at a brisk pace, although she knows she'll never be an Angelina Jolie look-alike. She also enjoys long walks outside when weather permits and will often borrow someone's dog, which provides a companion and is a great way to meet new people when they stop and say, "May I pet your dog?" Most recently, to stave off arthritis, she started doing floor exercises reminiscent of a high school calisthenics class to strengthen her leg and stomach muscles. Rita M. gained weight after her husband passed away. Although she had to dress up for work each day, she didn't care to shed the pounds. But four years after losing her spouse, she started remodeling both her second home or farm and herself. Jayne had always been proud of her figure, but after her second husband divorced her, she had gained weight. Once the divorce was imminent, she took charge and started to work out weekly with a trainer and eat better on her own.

Eat sensibly. Barbara knew it was time to get real. She was over 60, not some skinny teen. She started learning to love and concoct interesting salads, and eat more vegetarian meals. She hired a smart young couple to design her garden with a vegetable patch. Weeding also became another great daily exercise. Margaret, who enjoyed a daily menu of cookies, cakes, and anything chocolate, has learned these treats are okay in moderation. A high energy person, she is fortunate to have a turbo-charged metabolism. When she goes out, she often will eat only half her sandwich or dinner and take the rest home for the next night. This saves money and calories. In homage to better health, she has added more fresh veggies and fruits to her diet, some of which she now grows in pots during the summer on her screened in porch.

Shop for your age, but with some pizzazz. Barbara took a lump sum from her savings, with her financial advisor's blessing, and went to some wonderful shops where the saleswomen understood exactly what she wanted and were willing to spend time with her to find age-appropriate clothing with some zip that would complement her new figure. She also hit her town's lingerie shop for some new, sexier, nighttime wear, and got over the embarrassment of telling them she was dating and could no longer wear her flannel nightgowns. Also, she went through her closet and eliminated outdated items. Her new figure meant she could now fit into old, still-stylish clothing she had kept, which were classics with an Audrey Hepburn and Grace Kelly chic. One of her new, sexier outfits particularly pleased her when her mother said, "That doesn't look like your style." She replied with a big smile, "Absolutely! Exactly!" Margaret, who used to break out in welts at the thought of shopping, became comfortable frequenting certain clothing stores where salespeople left her alone so she wouldn't feel overwhelmed and could make her own selections, always heading for the sales rack first. In an ironic twist, her late mother would ask, "Where did you get that cute top? I love it." And she responded, "Want me to look for it in your size?"

Get therapy when you must. Barbara had signed up for enough therapy early on during the separation and the beginning of her divorce to understand who she was and what she needed to work on to make herself happy first, then others. She was determined not to make this a weekly necessity as she emerged from the shadows, but she also had become intuitive enough to realize she needed periodic boosters. She found an affordable local therapist who had top-notch credentials, engaged her in a conversation rather than passively nodding his head yes or no, had a sense of humor, didn't tell her what to do but listened, and weighed in and insisted she be brutally honest. They became a good team. He helped her through one poor relationship choice and to stick to her actions rather than wavering, a bad habit she picked up when she lost her confidence along the way. And he also rejoiced when she developed a healthy relationship with a good, stable man.

It's all about the neck. Nora Ephron said it brilliantly in her book, *I Feel Bad about My Neck*. Well, we do, too, Nora, and if you were still alive we could commiserate and laugh, and maybe get a 3-for-1 price from some prominent Park Avenue surgeon. We've started to see our necks sag and grow. To make matters work, we had always told everyone we would never do any kind of plastic surgery. How superficial, unimportant, and potentially dangerous, we said rather pointedly. We weren't one of those *Reality TV* women from Orange County or New Jersey. We also disliked some friends' work that had been done leaving them with crooked smiles, too tight skin so they couldn't smile or blink, and absolutely flat tummies. But then we started noticing plastic work everywhere—the same way pregnant or wannabe pregnant women see bulging bellies. We spotted tummy tucks, face-lifts, neck-lifts, and eye-lifts everywhere we went and then made peace with ourselves. We felt it was OK to be a bit superficial. When a designer friend from Los Angeles came to visit Barbara and asked if she noticed anything different, Barbara replied she didn't, yet told her friend that she looked the best ever. The friend smiled and informed Barbara that she had had a neck-lift, would share the surgeon's name, and offered Barbara a place to stay. Margaret insisted on getting in on the act. They had always done everything together, and Barbara wasn't going to have a tightened neck-line without her buddy. They made a pact to go together when they saved the dollars and built up their collective courage to go under the knife.

As we continue our quest to look well on the outside, with Barbara's occasionally backsliding due to not enough time to cook wisely and exercise sufficiently, or Margaret's insatiable craving for pastries and cookies, we know deep down that the internal us—our efforts to be good people in our behavior and the legacies we leave behind—are far more important than outside packaging. However, it sure is exhilarating to do our best on both fronts, even if remodeling ourselves we've found is tougher than any home self-improvement project we've ever tackled or written about.

12

HOME ON THE RANGE

MARGARET

SINGLE SERVING

As a child, I was not allowed in the kitchen, and my mother shouldn't have been allowed there, either. Mealtime for her was a chore. As a typical, stay-at-home, American mom in the '50s and '60s, she strived to feed our family home-cooked meals almost every night. We'd gulp down her culinary disasters and smile graciously, or chew and spit into our napkins if a dish was inedible. Having guests for dinner was a rarity. The few times my parents invited people to dine, my mother broiled lamb chops, roasts, or steaks until they were almost the color of mahogany. They were unimaginatively accompanied by baked potatoes or boxed macaroni and cheese, canned Brussels spouts, or asparagus.

When I first married, I had no idea how to cook. I had perfected three dishes that my best childhood friend and I would spend weekends concocting in her kitchen—cakes in various colors (using food coloring) and shapes; buttered popcorn; and Chef Boyardee, boxed, pizza mix that we'd top with little balls of hamburger. Not the best ingredients for a healthy diet.

My mother-in-law became my first cooking instructor. Her primary passion was creativity in the kitchen, adding a dash of this and that to her fabulous chicken soup made with a kosher chicken, lots of dill, root vegetables, and a tiny bit of ketchup for color, or perfectly seasoned and cooked brisket bathed in Kitchen Bouquet to give it a rich brown crust and color. I'd sit in her large cozy kitchen in amazement watching her effortlessly prepare thick vegetable-laden soups and meat casseroles that sent divine aromas wafting through her home and enticing hungry family members to hurry to her table.

Every day my father-in-law would walk to the Jewish bakery a block from their home and buy a fresh rye bread to accompany her delicious meal. My mother-in-law considered cooking a source of great pride and accomplishment, watching others enjoy the result of her latest creation—tonight a honey-roasted chicken with new red potatoes and fresh asparagus, or tomorrow meat-falling-off-the-bone short ribs with white beans simmered in sweet, red wine. She never baked, however. That was my sister-in-law's purview, which she did deliciously from scratch, never from a boxed mix.

Cooking and entertaining were out of my marital comfort zone. I broiled or grilled meats, prepared a boxed rice or noodle dish, and added a vegetable such as frozen peas, broccoli, or lima beans. Nolan had to have a salad with every dinner, and he would chop, mix, and toss iceberg lettuce, tomato, cucumber, and onion with Wishbone Italian dressing. How b-o-r-i-n-g. But what did we know back then?

We rarely entertained, and never in formal fashion. In fact, we preferred to have friends over to dine in our backyard by the pool. We dressed in jeans or shorts with a menu planned around my husband's favorite barbecued foods—roasted corn on the cob, hot dogs, and thick burgers served with baked beans, on paper plates, with plastic flatware and paper napkins. We did all together. He grilled, selected the right wines and beers, and we shopped for ingredients. I did the side dishes and often bought the dessert, made chocolate chip cookies (my one specialty), or asked someone to bring their choice.

However, after my husband died, I was ripe to have new adventures cooking as a single. To gin up for this new undertaking, I signed up for fancy cooking classes where I'd learn how to do such culinary pursuits as debone my own chicken breasts, a good skill to acquire.

Top on the list now that I was on my own was throwing my first ever formal dinner party—certainly not black-tie, but with hors d'oeuvres, a three-course meal, real silver, good china, and lots of good wine. I wanted to see if I could do it alone. I knew it would be a challenge, yet rationalized that it could be fun. I had more time once I retired from my full-time job, and I was living in my mother's spacious condo, which offered the perfect setting for a proper, sit-down, *Downton Abbey*–style repast. The downside would be the expense, perhaps a ruined meal where everybody would go home famished and gorge on what was in their refrigerators or never come back. At least I had tried.

Widow's Peak: Margaret's Tips on How to Throw Your First Formal Dinner Party

- Approach the task in an organized fashion and break it down into small parts. I selected a date on the calendar, but had to decide on the time and guest list. I took out a legal pad and planned all as I would a story. I started five weeks ahead and created a timeline. I would begin with the guest list, figure out a menu, cook as much as I could ahead of time so I wouldn't be stuck in the kitchen, do the setup, and then feed the guests after announcing, "Dinner is served."

- Consider the chemistry of those who would sit around my table. I was determined to shake up the usual cast of characters and include a few other singles. Food preferences had to be factored in with this one, a vegetarian who on occasion eats fish; another, a vegan and gluten-free eater; one with a peanut allergy; another who never eats red meat, but her husband is on the Paleo diet so go figure what they eat at home; and another who dislikes cooked green vegetables. I settled on 10 guests and sent an evite, followed up with a phone call for those who didn't RSVP quickly.

- Come up with a menu. I wanted to make it easy yet elegant, again without spending the evening trapped in the kitchen. Over the years, I have absconded with dozens of recipes from restaurants and online sources. Many have become standbys that I make when I invite a friend over for dinner—such as chicken raspberry from the *Silver Palate Cookbook*, a tomato sauce from Marcella Hazan's *The Classic Italian Cook Book*, or a pasta bolognaise from a *Sebastiani Family Cookbook* that carries an inscription from the family matriarch to my husband. I trawled other cookbooks for ideas. I turned to exotic cooking magazines, and an occasional celebrity tome for my main courses. I'd start with a simple salad of field greens and homemade balsamic vinaigrette. For the entrée, I wanted to cook something new, worthy of a top rating from a Michelin guide, but a recipe that wouldn't be a grind and made with ingredients available only at the city's specialty and expensive food markets. Choosing the right dish took almost more time for me to decide than preparing a tax return. Fortunately, I got a tip from the husband of someone I was interviewing for a story, who slipped me his favorite, foolproof dinner party recipe culled from a Napa Valley restaurant. It was grilled fillet of Pacific salmon with Thai red curry sauce and Basmati rice.

- Select the wines. This was a challenge to pair wines with Asian fare. The best combinations, which I discovered from writing about the marketing of wine and reading wine e-newsletters, are aromatic or fruity white wines or a Riesling with a hint of sweetness. Reds that tend to work best are a Syrah, Pinot Noir (my favorite), and many Rhones. I have a great local wine merchant and a daughter in the wine business to help with my choices. Part of the fun would be making the selections by going to tastings and sampling this and that.

- Choose a sweet ending. I pored over exhaustive directions about how to make a chocolate cake. Barbara suggested a divine, rich, chocolate cake that she had made repeatedly from Scott Peacock and Edna Lewis's Southern cookbook, *The Gift of Southern Cooking*. Barbara had eaten at Watershed, Peacock's restaurant in Atlanta, and raved. I gave it my twist by serving it with fresh raspberries and freshly whipped cream.

- Set the stage. This was crucial for my formal party. Fortunately, two days before the party, my sister, a younger version of entertainment guru Perle Mesta, was in town. She set the table with me lining up elegant, white, lace placemats and matching napkins across my gleaming wood table, gold napkin holders, blue-and-white Spode dishes, and a flower arrangement she suggested of white hydrangeas and tulips with blue-purple irises to complement the china. I used my mother's Waterford crystal and the sterling silver flatware I received as a wedding present.

- Get it together the day of. I spent most of the day cooking, took already-prepared dishes out of the freezer, and two hours before guests were to arrive, I vacuumed, puffed pillows, and dusted; washed and ironed the linen towels for the powder room, and made sure there was soap and plenty of tissues; and put out my favorite chocolates and nuts and napkins for the hot and cold hors d'oeuvres I would serve. I filled the ice bucket, set out the right wine glasses, chilled the white wines, and slightly chilled the reds. I turned on certain lamps, dimmed overhead lights, put new candles into candle-holders to add a dash of romance, and surveyed the scene. Lack of music was the one missing ingredient. I didn't yet have a sound system.

- Put the props in place when the first guests arrive. I handed each a glass of prosecco to loosen them up, a tradition my husband and I had observed, and that I wanted to continue as a way to include him in my first solo performance. I passed out hot mushroom tartlets and caramelized bacon, which I had prepared a few hours earlier, that matched well with the prosecco. I also placed on the coffee table three wedges of cheese from the Loire Valley my brother and his wife had sent me for the holidays.

- Move the party around. An hour after guests arrived, it was on to the dining room, where the conversation continued to flow. There were lots of "oohs" and "ahs" about my preparations, as well as some shock. "I didn't know you could cook, Margaret!" Several asked for recipes, which I promised to e-mail the next day. At the end of the meal, as we headed into the living room for coffee and other after-dinner drinks, everyone settled in comfortably. I took a mental snap-shot of the continued banter, the fact nobody had been eager to leave, and the realization that my first fancy dinner party had been a huge success.

Albeit exhausted, I was proud of my newfound expertise. Once was enough, I thought to myself as I crawled into bed a few hours later and threw the covers over my head, determined never to emerge, much less throw a formal dinner party again. Next time, I will slink back into my marital comfort zone of casual entertaining. Fortunately, there's a bar-becue grill in the condo courtyard.

BARBARA

FOOD AS DATING FODDER

Food has always loomed large in my life, from my suburban '50s childhood with a mother who considered from-scratch meals the benchmark of being a good wife and role model, to my carrying the mantle forward once I married. No quotidian Hamburger Helper or Rice-A-Roni for us (or rarely) after our early married years. Julia Child's books became my muse. My friends and I cooked obsessively from them, long before Julie Powell chronicled doing so in her book, which became the hit movie *Julie and Julia*.

Yet, before I got through the most labor-intensive recipes such as a homemade onion soup that required tearing up for hours, or exhaustive *boeuf bourguignon*, the *Silver Palate Cookbook* duo, Julee and Sheila, tempted me with simpler but still delicious recipes, such as chicken Marbella. That became one of our go-to, dinner-party favorites for years. Others encouraged me, too—Maida Heatter with her Queen Mother's chocolate cake—a favorite for flourless Passover desserts, Marcella Hazan for classic real-Italian pastas, Joyce Chen for Chinese wok-made dishes, and Martha Stewart with her oh-so-Martha-ish, tiny, stuffed cherry tomatoes and peapods—the beginning of seed-to-table cuisine.

In fact, food became the glue in many of our friendships and even our marital relationship, and my husband proudly encouraged me. But after 29 years, the embers of his passion for me waned, then died like a deflated chocolate soufflé, but without leaving a sweet taste in my mouth. Cooking mostly solo, once our daughters were off to college and then their own settled lives, held no interest. I tried recipes and cookbooks for singles—*Single Servings* and *Table for One*, which drove home more my alone status. Conversation was the missing ingredient. I craved shared banter about the preparation of a dish, dissecting what I had made, and how it could be improved. As a solo diner, I became the connoisseur of assembly-line cuisine—salads with an array of fixings or low-fat cottage cheese straight from the container, and all eaten hurriedly while standing at my kitchen counter with the TV on so there wouldn't be dead silence.

As I stepped into the dating world, not only were a man's use of proper grammar, truthfulness about marital status, finances, height, and political leanings critical, but so was how he felt about food and cooking. If he pooh-poohed the idea or always dialed for take-out or reservations, red flags shot up like Scud missiles.

Some, who were timid cooks for not having tried, still piqued my interest if they seemed trainable. Even those who got competitive and told me they knew how to make a better chicken Milanese atop arugula or penne à la vodka than I did, deserved an encore for raising the bar. The guy who loved my homemade compotes certainly stole my heart, and along with it, my seasonal produce. He lasted on and off for several years from summer blueberries and strawberries, through fall apples to winter cranberries and oranges, and then spring rolled around, and the cycle repeated itself, and I still was stirring for him. But I eventually had to dis him in part because he always was checking out two—or more—"cupcakes" simultaneously—other sweeties and me. I knew I deserved better than being in his dating bake-off.

When least expected, I was fixed up, the first since I had been divorced ten years before. We dined at a restaurant where I don't remember what we each ate, but recall the food and wine were good and the conversation nonstop. The second date was over great pizza. Another date with friends, and he confessed he was smitten. By the fourth date he was helping me cook at friends' home for an annual New Year's Eve dinner, and shared that his specialty was making salad with a dressing he learned from his French son-in-law. We had gone continental. We proved we could work a deux, and he didn't laugh when I said I loved reading cookbooks in bed. I asked a few friends and relatives for confirmation about this choice, but not my Greek chorus of closest pals and daughters as I used to do. My gut told me he was right. Everything was easy, even uncomplicated and fun.

Soon, he stepped into my small kitchen for the first time. I shuddered. I loved the recipe of cooking together, company, and live conversation, but having someone put my pots and pans away in the wrong cabinet or mess up how I stored my canned goods and spices made me wonder if I had lived on my own too long. I apologized profusely, kept saying the proverbial "I'm sorry," but couldn't let go of being territorial. When his son-in-law and daughter, with their baby daughter, visited from Paris and insisted on making all her organic food, I had to yield total control.

Once they left—and I found I had survived, it became easier. We loved preparing nice dinners, putting away our cell phones, and sitting down together to talk, sometimes on a Friday evening with a challah, wine, prayers, and Shabbat candles glowing.

Of course, our first disagreement—and biggest—was about food. It was over a brisket. He wanted to take charge and cook it in the oven followed by on the grill. It became overdone, tough—and almost inedible. I was annoyed. A first-cut brisket from my favorite butcher costs $7.49 a pound or so. He rescued the relationship, if not the brisket. "You don't want to look back and think we broke up because of a brisket, do you?" He was dead right. We moved on to mushroom barley soup, sweet potato fries, roast chicken with vegetables, and short ribs of beef cooked in good red wine. I regularly baked him my Woo–Chocolate Chip cookies with the best chocolate and southern pecans when he said he had never met a cookie he didn't like.

This time around there weren't expensive gifts that glittered or sparkled. Cookbooks, new salt and pepper mills, and an omelet pan became favorite ways to show we cared and mark milestones. The best gift was enthusiastically debating together whether to add more mayonnaise and dried cranberries to a broccoli salad from a favorite author, or more cheese and tomatoes to another chef's spicy bean tacos. We also made homemade pizzas with different toppings weekly and photographed them to share online. We reviewed on Yelp meals eaten out. When we each gained too many pizza pounds, we segued to wonderful colorful salads with everything from chopped broccoli to chick peas, orange segments, cranberries, almonds, and so on.

When we realized food was one of our prime conversation topics, we tried to dial it down and focus on more worldly, serious topics—the chance for marriage equality passing, which international airlines were safest, and the pros and cons of an increasing number of 2016 Presidential candidates. Yet, we always circled back to food. As we planned our first trip abroad, Fixup (the moniker I gave him, inspired by food writer Amanda Hesser and her Mr. Latte) and I started to drink more Italian wine and cook al dente. My younger daughter even asked me more than once, as Fixup took charge of more meals, "Mom, do you cook any more?" "Yes, of course," I reply, shooting her a snarky look. The way to my heart definitely has been through my range.

How to Cook with a Guy, Eat Together, and Not Spoil the Brisket or Relationship

We found ourselves on the learning curve, as we each stepped into the kitchen. Barbara was a co-chef for the first time and Margaret was finding her way as a solo chef who soon would be sharing her kitchen space with a partner. It takes time to feel comfortable cooking with another while each finds what each is best at doing, as well as not critiquing efforts with negative comments and focusing on the sharing, laughs—even mistakes. Here's our recipe that seems to work:

- Decide if you're ready. Cooking for a guy is a big message; you're asking him into your home with an open-ended timetable. Are you ready or want to encourage him to stay and linger? How do you plan to get him to leave, especially after two glasses of a great big Burgundy? Cooking at his home is an even bigger deal, since it can prove harder to get away because you have to get home, which, if you didn't drive, means you have to rely on your date. If at your home, you can politely say, "Please go."
- When cooking together, learn to banish the words, "my kitchen." Nobody needs to be reminded that it—and everything in it—is yours. Do you want to hear it's his at his place? But if you have some rules such as don't use that best copper sauté pan for an everyday omelet, speak up early and gently rather than harbor resentment.
- Decide in advance how you share food expenses when you're regularly cooking a deux—or you may become resentful when he uses all your expensive saffron or drinks all your Nespresso coffee, and doesn't pay for any groceries.
- Divide labor unless you really want to do all. Do you want to assume regular roles of chopper, sautéer, server, cleaner, or to ad lib as you go? Barbara is best at deciding on the recipes and handling the baking. Fixup likes to take charge of the shopping, preparing the salads and grill, choosing the wines, and cleaning the dishes. Margaret's new, regular partner fancies himself a su-

per chopper and, with his well-honed palate, will taste and add his suggestions to the dish at hand.

- Talk ingredients and brand labels. If you're intent on only eating expensive brands and he brings in generic items for a great price, are you willing to try his cheaper choices? Or are some stores' private-label brands fine, such as Whole Foods' 365 labels or Trader Joe's? Be honest and be open. Barbara and Margaret are sticklers for using really good ingredients.
- Discuss methods. If he likes to sauté sliced mushrooms in one layer slowly, then flip them over and do it again, and that drives you a bit bananas since you tend to toss them all into a pan willy-nilly, will that be a problem? Or should your rule simply be, you do it as you wish, and he does as he wants. So, hands off!
- Talk about measurements and following a recipe. Some cooks never sift flour, measure ingredients exactly, and adapt here and there for taste, which Barbara and Margaret have come to do more and more as they speed up the cooking process—even some of their baking. Others are intent on doing everything by the recipe book.
- Share menu ideas. Some think a meal means a first course, main course, vegetable, starch, salad, bread, and dessert every night of the week. Others are content with a great burger or BLT sand-wich and fries. When Barbara suggested the BLT menu, she was asked: What else? Where's the salad or side courses? It all comes down to expectations and communication, which need to be dis-cussed. Nobody is a mind reader.
- Talk messiness. Some chefs are clean-as-you-go freaks—put down your fork and it's off to the dishwasher. Others are let's do all at the end, or leave until tomorrow morning, or wait for the butler.
- Expand taste buds. A new relationship is a great time to broaden your tastes and ethnic cuisines except when you're allergic or just won't eat red meat, octopus, or raw-fish sushi, for instance. In those cases, is it OK to have separate meals? Or, is the more adventuresome resigned to being less adventuresome? Barbara's become an almost no-meat-eater, and she and Fixup have re-solved they eat by her taste buds at her home but when they go out, anything goes. If some guy just won't try vegetables, such as Margaret's partner, who won't eat anything green except haricots

vert (go figure, but maybe the French name has something to do with it), resist nagging. You're not going to change a seventy-year-old after sixty-nine years of no-green-things-on-my-plate-ever, please!

- Debate the pros and cons of nibbling while cooking. Some don't like anyone's fingers or forks taking a taste of a work in progress—and especially double dipping. Others think it's romantic to share anything and everything.
- Critique sweetly. Are you able to take some heat for your results, or not? If not, do you want to keep making the meatloaf the way your mother did when he has other ideas and leaves most on his plate? Again, share your criticism acceptance level and how you want him to dish it out. Same goes for him.
- Set the table. Are you happy eating at a counter with the TV on, or do you prefer sitting at the kitchen or dining room table with candles burning and cell phones off? Here's another topic of discussion in advance of sitting down: Margaret's partner has a rule. Do not clear any plates until everyone is through eating.
- Talk about leftovers. Some abhor them; others think nothing's better than brisket, chili, or coq au vin the next day, as flavors have merged. Margaret's late husband would never eat them, or quiche, or soup as a main course.
- To take home—or not, doggie bags and all. Decide how you feel if he wants to bring home the leftovers for his lunch or dinner the next day. Were you planning to reuse or freeze? Be honest. You're not in the restaurant business, yet.
- Inviting guests. Some love to cook for others and entertain. Others find it all a great hassle and stressful. Discuss this matter, too, as well as how you like to entertain—buffet or seated, and with the two of you preparing all or letting others bring some of the dishes. Also discuss who belongs together in the mix—your friends, his friends, some from each side, or those you've made together. If you are seating everyone, discuss the seating chart.
- Don't draw lines in the sand. This is only about cooking and eating, not figuring out how to make Putin love us, saving more women and children from terrorism in this country and abroad, and finding a way to improve our planet's climate. Always main-

tain your senses of humor. It's really not complicated, despite the movie with that title.

13

THE ELEPHANT IN THE ROOM: WHAT ABOUT S-E-X?

MARGARET

DATING? SEX @ 60+? SAY WHAT?

About a year after my husband died, people began asking me if I had met anyone. Even my attorney got in on the discussion. "Do you think you'll consider dating again?" I looked at him as if he had just suggested I participate in an orgy. He continued, "It's fine to live with someone, but I advise you not to get remarried. It might be too complicated legally in terms of your estate planning."

Dating? Remarried? I don't think so, I remember blurting out and thinking no way will I ever go out with another man or have sex with him. But was I being a prude? Just not ready.

Never say never.

I grew up in the halcyon '50s and '60s, when nice girls kept boys at arms' length and those who didn't and got in trouble were labeled "easy." I hadn't dated since before I was married in 1968. I was a very late bloomer and had gone out with only two boys in high school and a few more in college. Let me add, those were the days when girls lived in all-girls dorms and boys in all-boys dorms, and there even were curfews.

Few of us had sex, and if we did, it was with a serious boyfriend or someone we intended to marry. The tipping point in most relationships was when the boy said, "I love you." I remember having a roommate, who was mad for some boy. He told her the three magic words and voila! got her pregnant. She had a backstreet abortion and was sick after it for a month. I was mortified and would never have allowed myself to get into that position. Sex would be reserved for marriage. It was safer that way.

Fast forward forty-two years and the mores, I discovered, had been flipped around. Today, there is something wrong with women if they don't have sex, whether on the first date, just for the pure physical pleasure, or on a subsequent date, if they're in a relationship or like the person. Men and women living together has become de rigueur, something that was taboo back in my former dating days.

Naturally, dating and sex became topics of conversation at our grief support meetings among the widows who mostly were in their 50s and 60s. Robin was already having a passionate liaison with a good-looking Italian man she met at an outdoor festival. The sex was great, she reported, and *mamma mia* he loved to cook for her. I jokingly labeled him her "Italian Stallion." We were all ears living vicariously as she discussed the details of her new relationship. I remember nudging Pat, who was sitting next to me in the group and whispering, "That will never be us. I'd rather have root canal without Novocain."

Again, never say never.

When Nolan died, I not only lost a good friend but I lost touch—no more hugs, kisses, and intimacy. The absence of sex was fine. I had adjusted to that. We hadn't been intimate throughout his entire illness. I had many friends and dates with them and my work kept me busy enough. I was in a pretty good routine.

Then one day when I was in an Apple store getting my iPhone fixed, out of the corner of my eye I saw a man staring at me. About 15 minutes later, it registered. Hey that was R. who I dated in high school. (I must explain here that I have an amazing memory for faces that I cultivated in my work as a reporter and photographer.) When I turned around to find him to say, "Hello," he was gone. I relayed the incident to one of my sisters who said, "Track him down and send him an e-mail. Maybe he's single."

"Oh, I don't do that kind of thing," I said. Barbara, now the voice of dating experience, encouraged me, "Meg, don't be such a prude. It's a new world. Meet him for coffee. It's good dating practice. You're not marrying him."

I did some sleuthing, found his e-mail address, and contacted him only to discover that he lived less than two miles from me. It seemed impossible that our paths had never crossed. Friends joked that I couldn't even find a guy from a different zip code. And, he was single.

We met late one spring afternoon. The conversation flowed easier than the unpalatable cabernet I was gulping to give me confidence. I found out what he had been doing for the last 50 years. We talked for three hours until I had to go meet my eldest son for dinner. "This was nice," he said as we hugged and said goodbye. "Contact me again some-time," he added. I don't know where this surge of confidence came from but I replied, "No, now it's your turn."

He called. We started going out. After one of our first dates in a lovely restaurant, I flew out of R.'s car when he brought me home, thinking I would break his arms if he even tried to kiss me goodnight. But did I owe him a roll in the hay to pay him back for a delicious meal of trout almandine, haricot verts, and two glasses of an earthy pinot noir? I didn't have a clue how to date, and, of course, was conflicted about the sex part. Barbara, who considered herself now the Dr. Ruth of the 60-plus set, relayed that sex was expected after three or so dates. That couldn't apply to me, I rationalized. I lost the love of my life and in my mind, if I had sex with another man, I didn't know how I would mitigate the guilt.

On the other hand, I found it really fun being with a guy who was safe, smart, and funny and with whom I had a history. I knew him and his family and was pretty sure he didn't have women tied up in the basement. Anyway, he didn't have a basement. It was comfortable and pleasant also to find someone again who thought I was terrific and attractive, liked me for me, and was willing to give me the space to discover my new independent side.

We went out as friends for nearly four months before the subject of sex hit the fan. He had hinted a few times; I ignored that part of the conversation. He was trying to be patient because I had lost my spouse. I discussed the sex part with my grief counselor. What if? How? I don't know if I can. I have to do what? She encouraged me to try. Intimacy was wonderful, she said. I told her he had dated dozens of women over the years; some were also my friends. I had very little experience. Her response, "Just imagine how much experience he has had." My eyes popped out. What! Wow! She then suggested, if I take the plunge, to set the boundaries with him in advance—was he checked for STDs, could he be monogamous, and did he even want to have an intimate relationship with me? Hmmm.

I also discussed this with some of my closest old friends, my new grief support pals, and with an acquaintance, Kimberly, who I met in a class. She was divorced and a seasoned dater. I even brought up the subject with my dental hygienist, Ginny. (Try talking about this subject with dental tools in your mouth.) Her response to what words she could understand was: "Margaret, don't be rash. Companionship is great. My middle-aged friends would give anything to meet a wonderful sweet man their age."

I had many things to consider if I did succumb to S-E-X: Did my parts even still work? Would it hurt post menopause? Would he expect to see me nude? Would I even enjoy it at my age? It had been eight years. How do you have sex at such an old age with an old body? Was sex okay with someone you just dated, without having a long-term commitment? And what would he think of me? Would I be labeled a senior slut? Oh, why not, I finally figured. This was my new life.

So one night I mustered the courage to have the talk. Did R. want to remain friends or take our relationship to the next level? I allowed him to choose door 1—platonic friends, 2—we go out but date others, or 3—be exclusive. "Next level or door 3," he said without taking a breath. About a week later after attending the opera *Madame Butterfly* with another couple, R. turned to me and said, "Do you want to spend the night?" I stammered and then said, "Sure" and went home with him. In the car on the way to his apartment, my mind was buzzing. What should I wear? I had nothing to wear—and that (nude) wasn't an option. He threw me one of his T-shirts. And then he set the scene. I felt like I was playing a role in some cheesy Lifetime TV movie and started to giggle. I always laugh when I'm nervous. He lit candles, turned on Frank Sinatra and Barbra Streisand, or what I consider make-out music, and the rest just happened naturally. He was very considerate and slow, checking out how I was feeling along the way.

Of course, when I got home the next day I immediately went on the Internet to read more about sex after sixty. Yeah, seniors were doing it and having fun. In some ways, sex with him was better than when I was younger. It was sweet and gentle—neither of us was in a rush to check on the kids or worried about pregnancy or interruptions. Sex later in life and with the right person is a bonus because men and women need more time to relax and get in the mood. I am happy to report, my parts worked very well indeed.

For months, I was in the closet about dating, let alone having sex. I felt so torn, as if I were cheating on Nolan. It took almost a year for me to feel comfortable enough to admit that I was part of a new couple. For forty-two years, it had been "Meg and Nolan." Now it was Meg and someone else, and who knows for how long? For now I can truly say that it's a wonderful indulgence to spend time with a kind, considerate man who, when I can't sleep, will massage my shoulders and sing me his favorite lullabies. Or I can sit with him in a warm, comfortable room with a fire blazing on a snowy winter's day. I enjoy his company and know that I can be sexy, have strong feelings for another man, and most important, smile, and laugh again.

BARBARA

MANY TOADS BEFORE A BIG LEAP

It was a subject I never talked about when I was happily married. None of my friends did, except, maybe, to ask whether I had ever had an affair, or contemplated one. No to both questions, but I probably wouldn't tell if I had. I was raised conventionally. Nice girls didn't talk about this subject, or venture out of the marriage. In fact, when one writing colleague asked me if she could interview me about my sex life for an article and would promise anonymity, I quickly replied, "Absolutely, not. It's not something I share, ever!"

And why would I? I thought my marital intimacy was normal, whatever that meant, given our busy careers, life with two teenage daughters with bedrooms close by, decades of marriage, and slightly different notions about what was typical in the bedroom—especially in a long-term marriage and at our advanced ages. According to Dr. Oz, for married couples between the ages of fifty to fifty-nine, the frequency is about once a week. We passed. And as most of us know, men and women don't agree eye to eye, or relate different stories, given Diane Keaton and Woody Allen's different responses in the movie *Annie Hall* to the questions about how much and how satisfying the amount of sex was. For him, it wasn't enough; for her, it was plenty.

For me it wasn't about quantity, but the quality, and greatly about having someone appeal to me and vice versa. I went on the offensive. I prepared for when the opportunity might hit. Little did I know I needed to ramp up the learning curve quickly. So many men's online profiles talked about wanting good chemistry, which to me meant a physical attraction and sex. Some were quite blunt and said they liked sex, and it mattered a lot in a relationship, along with lots of kissing.

In addition, so many of the books I read while sitting on the floor in the self-help section of bookstores and libraries addressed intimacy bluntly: when to go to bed with a partner, how to make yourself sexually appealing, what made intimacy good for each—or bad, what positions worked and didn't, and so on. I even bought *Real Sex for Real Women* by female sexual authority Dr. Laura Berman, with detailed descriptions and photographs in color, since I considered myself quite inexperienced. Most of our mothers had urged us to wait until we met someone we loved and even might marry to hop into the sack. The guys would be our teachers since they were supposed to be experienced. I had one friend whose mom had lost her husband and remarried, and seemed very avant-garde—perhaps, Bohemian—in encouraging a healthy sexual life for her daughters, and even granddaughters.

I believed intimacy would come up at some distant time when I met someone I was crazy about. Wrong, I learned after talking with an Internet acquaintance, who became a friend when he started to date another woman before we could meet. He sought me out as a confidante and asked over the telephone for help with his sex life: "What do you think?" he said, "I've gone out with this woman several times and we've not yet been intimate?" I replied, "How would I know. I'm not in a relationship, let alone dating. I'm still shopping online." I promised as a diligent reporter to help. It was good information for me, too.

I asked my older, college-age daughter if there were rules my generation should know. "It's expected by the sixth date," she said, matter-of-factly. It seemed to be the expectation for someone who was divorced. Most men would give more space and time to someone who had lost a spouse.

I counted on my fingers; that meant probably six weeks if one date per weekend, or if two dates a weekend, maybe three weeks. I relayed this to my Internet friend, and we decided that his trip to Paris with his honey would produce the right romantic opportunity. It did, but I think at that point it was the eighth or ninth date.

In the meantime, I panicked about the timetable and wondered if my daughter and her friends were correct, or only about the twenty-something set. When I last dated—in the late '60s, three or six times was the minimum I usually waited to kiss someone goodnight. The sexual revolution, which so many of my friends experienced who hadn't married as soon as I had in 1971, totally passed me by.

To catch up, I started to ask others and garner tips about how best to set the mood, what to wear, what guys liked at this age in bed, and so on. Some friends said they heard that no sex by the third date was a deal breaker. Others informed me that sexy lingerie, little boy shorts with a nonathletic T-shirt, or a guy's big pajama top à la Annette Bening in the movie *The American President* were the requisite uniforms. Several others said that it was important to have a serious conversation before-hand about whether we were going to be exclusive, and even to show proof with medical papers that neither of us had an STD, or to be so bold as to purchase condoms and keep them in a purse or night table.

It seemed to be getting so complicated and sounded less romantic, yet necessary. However, other matters disturbed me far more. I was in my fifties, had had two children by Caesarean section with a nice big horizontal scar as a reminder, had gained some pounds (that I hadn't completely removed) during and after my divorce proceedings, had a few varicose veins, and never had had a Brazilian wax job. In addition, my boobs were sagging, I wasn't interested in cosmetic surgery, and was never one to parade around naked, even with my female friends or daughters at a spa or on vacation, or when they visited my home. I decided pitch blackness would be my camouflage. I hadn't yet figured out what I would do come morning and bright sunlight.

A friend put the positive spin on the situation. "Look how lucky you'll be. You don't want to die with having had only one sexual partner. You've got a wonderful adventure ahead of you," she said in her always comforting, nonjudgmental tone.

Yes, so true, but that first time. I didn't have the conversation mem-orized that actress Candice Bergen offered when she and businessman/

real estate developer Marshall Rose were getting serious, which she relayed in her second memoir, *A Fine Romance*. "One night I told him, 'You know, Marsh, what I'd really love is to read the Sunday papers with you.' The next morning I watched him shave for the first time; we read the papers in bed'" (Bergen 2015, p. 223). I knew the *New York Times* paper was important for a reason beyond knowing all the news!

I was pleasantly surprised how well I handled the transition from dumped to dating diva, though it took time and humor. I went to my favorite lingerie shop, hesitated a bit, then told the owner I needed something new and sexy. She got it immediately and helped me pick out a short, sleeveless, raspberry colored nightgown with a deep V for cleavage to show, when the moment arose. Flirting came easily whether in e-mail banter, on the phone, or in person. It was almost like getting on a bicycle again. I found I handled keeping my distance when somebody didn't appeal, and I didn't care if he thought me frigid if I didn't want to kiss upon meeting or parting—or more—as so many men had. They seemed to think a smooch was obligatory.

I also found I liked when someone I was attracted to took my hand, put his arm around me warmly, kissed me, and even better, made out with me like we were starry-eyed teens. I no longer felt I was back in high school and had to worry about being termed a slut, or worse. I could throw out my old rule book about intimacy. I wasn't worried about getting pregnant; had raised two terrific daughters; felt good about my career, relationships with family and friends; loved my longer hair with highlights; and didn't have to explain anything to my mother. Or, did I? I debated having a talk with her as time progressed. Here's how it was going to go: "Mom, you know I have been married, had kids, and this is the new normal when someone stays over or I stay over at his place." I decided she would understand and wanted me to have a full-blown, healthy relationship again. We never had that talk.

And here's the real scoop, censored a bit. I knew I could have sex casually if I wanted—opportunities were plentiful—but I discovered that my internal gut was still old-fashioned enough to require me to like the guy and think our togetherness had some legs—not a forever, but some longevity. I also had to find him attractive—in personality, looks, smarts, humor, and kissability—what chemistry came to mean to me. I also found I didn't have to be in love—far from it.

The first time—a year after I was separated and my former husband had filed for divorce—it was easy when the guy told me how sexy he found me. How could I resist after being spurned. In the dark, I undressed and crawled under the sheets. He asked if it was the first time post-separation. I lied and said, "Of course, not." I didn't want him to feel pressure, but I insisted on protection as Margaret had advised me, which annoyed him. The experience was unmemorable, except for re-testing my equipment and finding it worked, despite my post-menopausal concerns. The next time was with another guy I had e-mailed and talked to so much that by the time we met, it felt like the tenth date. The intimacy was terrible. We didn't click.

Along the way, with a new, short, black, sleeveless nightgown with lace, I found that most guys loved oral sex, didn't like much chit-chat—they're not as good as women about multitasking; that they all are immodest, that some needed a boost from Viagra or Cialis, and that they also might encounter failures that had nothing to do with me, but aging and ED (erectile dysfunction); that some were selfish and all was about their bravado and showmanship, while others were very concerned about me and my fulfillment. With some positive reviews (which I declined to share on Yelp), I learned to find my voice and speak up when one wanted to shower together afterward—not my style I said—and when I was also in the mood more than the guy. In general, I came to love the entire experience with someone I really cared about and who cared about me, especially cuddling in the middle of the night and morning, and being able to laugh in bed about who knows what! I could even talk about anything related without hesitating when close friends asked (and they did), but in sweet, rather than prying, ways, "How's the chemistry?"

I still resisted when acquaintances inquired, however, which many also did. When the married wife of one of my former husband's law partners ran into me at a women's clothing store, she asked if I had a boyfriend, yet. I said, "Yes," and she quickly asked what it was like to be intimate again, since she said, sadly, she and her husband no longer were. I smiled and said nothing more. I didn't know her and wasn't going to share how great intimacy could be, though I felt sad for her. There were more small romances where it wasn't so good. One, in fact, was the worst experience I had ever had.

When others, and then Fixup, walked into my life, all the ingredients came together for the best kind of intimacy—chemistry, respect, sweetness, smarts, and fun. Months later when a good friend said over dinner that she couldn't wait until she reached a certain age to be able to forgo sex with her husband, whom she loved, and looked at me for confirmation, I smiled but decided honesty was the best policy. "Don't look at me," I said. "We're new to our relationship and enjoying all parts." I felt bad for her, but I felt glad that for me the elephant in the room had vanished. I still like to undress in the dark, however. Some things never change.

REFERENCE

Bergen, Candice. 2015. *A Fine Romance.* New York: Simon & Schuster.

14

SINGLE AND PLANNING FOR PERPETUITY

MARGARET

GOING UNDERGROUND

At one time in real estate parlance, if things were "moving down," we'd be referencing our basements. After my husband passed away four years ago, the term "moving down" took on new meaning—that is, going underground. It came to the fore as I searched hurriedly in a crisis for the right plot that would become his final resting place. I was totally in the dark about how to purchase this type of real estate.

Married for forty-two years, we both had been in denial about our mortality. Even after my husband became ill, we didn't discuss how we envisioned our funerals or how and where we wanted to be buried. We lived life as if it would go on forever, a typical boomerish response. That fantasy was derailed when my husband didn't beat his cancer. Our lack of planning smacked me hard in the face. I had no idea what I was supposed to do.

Unlike Nolan and me, Shelley M. and her late husband, Steve, had a perpetuity plan. It happened serendipitously. One day, Steve's parents gathered their sons together and said they were buying a family plot at a cemetery more than thirty minutes away from their home. When Steve came home to discuss it, Shelley, who was only in her 40s at the time, nixed the idea. First of all, she thought, "Gosh, I'm too young to be thinking about this now." However, since her in-laws broached the subject, Steve and Shelley talked about buying plots in a place closer to their home to make it easier for their one daughter to visit them some day. It's also where Shelley's parents were to be buried. Their decision to buy plots was fortuitous and saved Shelley from having to do this after her husband passed away of a rare neurological disease. Shelley asked Steve, who died in his sixties, if he wanted to be buried with his wedding ring and he said, "Yes." They also buried him with a train magazine—he was a train enthusiast—and their daughter's stuffed Pooh bear.

Joan and her husband Mike didn't initially have a plan. She decided when he went into the hospital with an illness that seemed terminal that she wanted to find out what kind of funeral and burial he preferred. Mike said he wanted a wake, mass, and to be cremated. After he died five weeks later, Joan asked his brother to pick up the ashes from the funeral home. He kept them for about a year before Joan felt "brave enough to think about what to do with them," she recalls. "When I did, I followed Mike's wishes to dump them in water; he loved water more than land. We put most of them, but not all, in a biodegradable pillow. Mike's brother and my son got in a canoe, paddled out, and put the pillow in the lake. My son said that the water swirled under the pillow in a way that he knew Dad was pleased. We gathered on a dock with family and friends for a ceremony where my children and I spoke about Mike. Then family members and friends shared 'Mike stories.' Later, I put some of his ashes in the ocean at our time-share in Florida. I went there with my sisters and just walked out in the ocean and dropped some quietly, early in the morning before there were many beachcombers. I 'talked' with him and walked down to our favorite breakfast place on the beach and spent some more time 'chatting' with him. In addition, each of my children took some of the ashes to scatter in their own yards."

I knew that going underground wasn't for everyone, but I was pretty sure my late husband would have turned in his grave if I had chosen to bury him above ground in a mausoleum (like my parents, who had decided to be buried in a crypt). I knew he also wouldn't want to be cremated, with his ashes placed on my nightstand like one widow I knew. After mulling all this over at the lowest point in my life, I shopped for cemetery plots, which could have a certain element of green cachet, depending on the location.

All was so different than when we had bought our home. Thirty-seven years before, when we moved back home, we worried about space for storage, windows, walk-in closets, enough bedrooms, and bathrooms for our three kids, a decent kitchen, good plumbing, and where to put the washer and dryer equipment.

This real estate would have none of these amenities. It probably wouldn't have much of a lawn, something my husband loved to mow, or real flowers that he enjoyed planting. Cemeteries in my area were crowded. Real estate for the departed was at a premium, and only going up in price. Who would have thought?

Although I am a journalist used to researching everything from wine to family businesses, real estate, and design, I didn't have the time or energy to check out options. I had to do this hastily and picked a plot in the zip code I knew he preferred. His plot also had to be on an aisle, the location he wanted for movies and airplane flights, and a good view was mandatory.

As upset and sad as I was at the time, I imagined a half grin on his face as I ticked off these requirements to the cemetery caretaker. The caretaker, in turn, suggested that I not just buy one plot but mine as well, cautioning me that all plots were going up in price—supply and demand—and might not be available if I waited. "I can always buy it back if you don't want it," he said. What a deal. And, then he tried to encourage me to buy more for my children.

I also had to select the location or our row. I opted to be in the neighborhood near my best friend's father and brother, knowing that my friend and the rest of her clan would be buried with them some day. My friend's folks bought plots, too, for her, her husband, sister, and sister-in-law. In this way, the person and her family who I spent the most time with growing up would be near my husband and me in perpetuity. We'd be nearly side by side resembling bookends, which is exactly the way we're photographed in so many of our school photos.

As the sun rose like a hot air balloon on that clear mild April morning one day after Nolan's death, I stood on the sidewalk of the cemetery negotiating my purchase, then writing a big check. I was in shock not only because I had just lost the love of my life, but also because how could I really be sure these subterranean spaces were escalating in price as suggested. I was in no place emotionally, however, to haggle. I just wanted the deed done.

As I turned to leave, I thought, "I hope I did well by you, Nolan. I'll join you one day and like all the years I slept beside you, I'll be back." I selfishly wished that it wouldn't be for a long time since I still, even in my great despair, hoped that someday I would again enjoy life while I could.

BARBARA

THE DIRT ON EXTREME DOWNSIZING

We boomers have carefully planned most of our real estate moves—starter apartments and homes to get on the equity upswing, and places to live as we raised families with good schools nearby and "location, location, location" our guiding mantra. Some of us even sought a larger home if we wanted to trade up, and now many of us are considering a place to trade down or downsize as we start to discard too many furnishings and possessions, and simplify our lives—including financially. Being single after my long-term marriage ended in divorce and giving up my former family home proved a great incentive for me to do all this.

Few of us, including myself, had thought ahead to our ultimate resting place. Why would we? Like other boomers who are active and healthy, we plan to live forever, and not just in our dreams, or so we think.

I never gave the idea much thought until my first grandson was born in 2014—handsome and healthy. Yet, the night he arrived, I couldn't stop crying and the tears weren't just from happiness. Suddenly, my mind did a flip-flop, and for the first time I was face-to-face with my mortality. Would I live long enough to witness all the wonderful milestones in his life—first steps and words, recognizing me at sight and on FaceTime or Skype, kindergarten, prom, graduations, confirmations, Bar Mitzvah, first love, and if lucky, his wedding day?

When I shared my concerns, friends questioned my sanity. Who thinks like that at such a deliriously gleeful time, they shot back, especially because longevity seemed on my side. My mother still lived alone, then at age ninety-four and a half; my dad had died, but lived until almost age eighty, when Alzheimer's stole him away in more ways than one.

I have always been a relentless planner, thinking ahead and organizing for important events. I have turned in most articles ahead of time. Now, with the birth of my grandchild and new grandmother status, I realized I had a new concern. I had dropped the ball. No longer was I young. I would not live forever. Moreover, since I was single, I neglected to realize there were worse things than a dateless Saturday night or New Year's Eve. Being alone in perpetuity trumped that. In this case there were many possibilities I'd have to weigh on my own: a casket; an in- or above-ground, vault, crypt for two, or mausoleum for many; or cremation—and then whether to invest in a special urn and inter it, ask one of my children to consider taking it for their mantel or trade it back and forth, or scatter my ashes. And then where?

I wasn't sure if the same rules applied that I had mastered when buying various houses and writing so much about real estate and design. Would "location" still be the benchmark, since resale wasn't an issue? Should I first search possibilities online? What about a corner lot? That might mean more noise and less privacy.

I didn't know, but understood clearly, the economics of supply and demand: With real estate at a premium, good cemeteries were filling up and prices for gravesites kept climbing. It was crunch time. I needed to put down a deposit, or, maybe, full asking price. But where?

My parents' family plot was in a bucolic cemetery in suburban New York, where many area temples owned land. While I wouldn't be in the same suburb where I grew up, at least I could be side by side with my father and near family friends who played significant roles in my life— Poldi, Lillian, Frances, Sandy, Fred. The list went on and on. The glitch? There was no room for me in their final "neighborhood." All four plots my parents purchased decades before were spoken for, and I disliked the idea of being rows away.

I asked my closest childhood circle, all boomers, about their plans. I kept hearing the same response: What plans? Susan, a friend from second grade, who resided in upstate New York, said she and her husband weren't sure. Her parents occupied slots in a family mausoleum in another suburban New York cemetery, with her mother sandwiched between her two husbands. She didn't think there was room for them there, let alone me. But she'd ask her older sister who might know.

David, a friend since kindergarten, said his parents were at the same cemetery as my dad but in a different temple lot. He graciously explained there was room for me, but he and his wife might not be interred there. Since they lived in California and his wife wanted to be cremated, he didn't expect to return east. While his parents were lovely, without him nearby, it didn't seem the best fit.

I thought about asking Xenia, another friend from kindergarten, but she wasn't Jewish, and most cemeteries still were segregated—something possibly to change, but not now. It probably couldn't happen soon enough.

I decided it was time to think outside the box. I asked Margaret about whether there was room where she had buried Nolan, and where she would be some day. After all, I had lived in their same city for 23 years until I relocated back east. I still loved it and returned once a year to work with her or visit good pals. Moreover, we did so much else together—wrote articles and books, celebrated Bar and Bat Mitzvahs, toasted weddings, and sadly, observed deaths. She said I could join them, but wondered: "Your kids will never visit you; won't that bother you?" I replied, "With their busy lives in other cities, they see me alive mostly for holidays and family vacations. When your children visit you, they can say 'hi' to me, too. And this is the town where I lived for so long and had mostly happy memories except my divorce." I was almost convincing myself.

Before finalizing in my mind that I might be shipped back to the Heartland, I asked Fixup, since we expected to be together for the long term, what he preferred for himself or for us. Although he lived in another city, we had become a pair—celebrating events, enjoying nothingness, and making our list of the fifteen trips we wanted to take before we died. He replied in his sweet, accommodating manner, "I'm game for any place you are, as long as it's not cremation. Below ground and by your side would be great." I felt better. We were in this together, too, and had the beginnings of a concrete perpetuity plan.

Then, I asked a local friend, Maureen, who co-owned a favorite store in my village, about her plans. She was from Chicago, but had lived so long in our East Coast 'hood that I reasoned she might prefer to remain . . . forever. She suggested we gather an interesting, diverse group of friends, including her business partner and husband. It sounded like the equivalent of one of our lively dinner gatherings. Her shop even sold chic placemats, dishes, glassware, cutlery, candleholders, candles, and more to make it festive. It also had the appropriate engraved stationery for our three collective daughters to send out condolence notes after we passed.

That said, it was time to find land: a water (Hudson River) or mountain (Catskill) view, space so nobody was on top of another, shade trees for hot summer sun and our area's glorious fall colors, and within walking distance of the small village we had come to love. A savvy real-estate salesperson could make a killing, if he or she found us the listing. He might even want in. We'd be sure to find a large enough plot. Death was no time to start being cliquey or exclusive. The more the merrier.

15

NEVER A GUARANTEE

Why do some marriages and relationships last and others crater? Was it luck or are some people far smarter in pairing up? In many respects, whether a marriage or partnership works can be a crapshoot. When so many baby boomers married young, even at age twenty-two to age twenty-five or so, maybe it was a little bit of this and that. In Margaret's case, she and her husband grew up together, but did not grow apart. As a result of our long marriages, we each came to understand that certain characteristics, behaviors, and circumstances definitely helped as we thought about our relationships, learned from our mistakes and those of our spouses, focused on the wonderful parts, and observed others' relationships and marriages—both healthy and not.

All marriages have their ups and downs. Joan S., who met Mike when they were teenagers and dated eight years before marrying, said she got more excited to be with him as they got older. "Mike was so positive, so caring. He had a laugh that lit up a room, and had a passion for life that was infectious. He was adventurous and fearless, jumped out of airplanes, loved motorcycles, yet had balance as a calm peaceful person. I'm intense. His presence was very calming and made me feel all was right with the world," she recalls. And, she adds, the two could talk about anything.

Sue W. married her best friend's brother when she was in her thirties. He passed away four years ago from cancer. "We were always in love. Our fights were brief and silly over such mundane things as the proper raising of our cats. (We never had children.) It was minor bickering, not major fights. And Steve believed in not going to bed angry. We were very close and best friends who finished each other's sentences," said Sue.

Each of us wanted to find a new lasting relationship, but also recognized, after our long journeys, that we could be alone if we didn't meet the right person. We worked hard to get to that point. We also knew that it was far better to be alone than with someone when the relationship didn't work, and when we felt we were forcing it or fantasizing that it would change. Those situations create even greater loneliness we found.

These are the ingredients we consider most essential for joyful togetherness.

Do not

1. ignore yourself. Look good for yourself and each other, which includes putting flannel nightgowns or pajamas and Granny jeans in mothballs or giving them to Goodwill.
2. get annoyed with each other about unimportant stuff. Also try not to get annoyed even about some important stuff. Learn to explain your feelings calmly, and use "I," rather than "you," messages.
3. use sarcasm and meanness. You can't take words back sometimes; even apologies won't always work.
4. bring up issues from the past. Keep discussions and arguments to one subject at a time rather than fill the kitchen sink. Exception: If you need to point out why something currently going on is too much of the same that already has happened.
5. make generalized statements. Be specific. "You look best when you wear checks rather than horizontal stripes." "Blue is a great color on you." The underlying message: I love you no matter what, even in that horrid, short-sleeved, button-down shirt, or in that too-tight-fitting dress.
6. criticize. If you do, say it lovingly and in a constructive way: "I love that you made dinner and, just so you know, the trash can is under the sink." Never ever criticize or shout in front of others. It's embarrassing for your loved one and the others.
7. be a backseat driver or Monday-morning quarterback. This is especially true when you're sitting in the front passenger seat.

8. always talk. Listen, and try not to get defensive. Show that you have listened by repeating back occasionally something said to you.

9. expect the moon, sun, and stars, particularly a Brady Bunch family. It's great if you each have children and grandchildren and everyone acts like one happy family, but that won't always be the case. Grown children may not like each other or be envious of new loves when they don't understand there's no finite amount of caring. Joan and Mike No. 2 have four children between them, each of whom accepted their relationship at their own pace. All four are now supportive. Do your best to encourage respect among all family members, but don't expect close friendships always to be forged automatically. Sometimes, it happens with time; sometimes it never does. Learn to set boundaries regarding the other person's existing relationships.

10. forget why you fell in love. Talk about those early days to recapture those early feelings when you go through a rough patch, or even when things are going great and you become a bit nostalgic.

Do

1. surprise each other with extravagant and cheap gifts for no reason. They can say in an important way, "I was thinking about you."

2. go out alone on dates at least once a week or month. Go without other couples, your children, and parents.

3. go on vacations alone and leave the kids behind, at least once a year. If you don't have lots of time; try to go away for a long weekend.

4. create fun evenings. Be playful and have fun with each other, laugh and more. Use humor to defuse stressful moments.

5. switch roles. Do something the other person usually does—plant flowers, clean the kitchen, take out the trash, rake leaves, empty the dishwasher, mow the lawn. Don't share that you're doing it, just do it.

6. say it if you have a problem. Your partner isn't a mind reader. Don't suppose your partner knows how you feel about all or anything unless you speak up.

7. be empathetic. You each need this in a sharing relationship when you have a problem.

8. ask for some space if you need it. Candace Bergen was good at doing this when she found Marshall Rose, her new spouse, was suffocating her with always telling her where he was going and what he was doing and that he wanted to be together 24/7.

9. make a ritual of going to sleep together. Say "I love you" and snuggle before falling asleep. Romance doesn't start at the bedroom door as one former date of Barbara's told her.

10. admit it and ask for forgiveness when you make a mistake. Take blame and responsibility. Learn to apologize fully with no "buts," and sometimes even if you weren't the one to start the argument or bad mood.

11. take long walks hand in hand. Get a dog to encourage this activity.

12. find activities to do together. It usually doesn't matter what— such as bridge, golf, concerts, drinking, appreciating wines and beers, cooking, museum going, movies, gardening, sailing—the sky's the limit. You don't have to do all together, but you should have a few activities you enjoy sharing.

13. respect. Say how wonderful he or she is at least once a day, and add how much you love him as well.

14. say "thank you" to your spouse or partner. Doesn't matter what it's for—taking you to dinner or for doing something that is special to you. It shows you're not taking each other for granted, and he's likely to return the favor and thank you as well.

15. get together at the end of the day. At fifty-plus, you probably don't have to prove yourself career-wise and burn the midnight oil nightly. The kids are probably gone and busy in their own lives. Save chatty phone calls with friends for daytime. Have a cocktail or even nonalcoholic beverage together before you cook or head out to dinner. Talk about the day and what's transpired, even if you spent the day together. Take Marshall Rose's advice from Candice Bergen's recent autobiography. "The whole point is to be with a person as much as possible." Consider the other person's point of view. Bergen didn't need 24/7 togetherness. They compromised.

16. find cute names or any name for each other. People may refer to him as your friend, significant other, life partner, honey, sweetie, beau, boyfriend, or just by his name. You each decide what's most comfortable and share it. Rejoice in your making these and other kinds of decisions together.

EPILOGUE

Broken Parts and Hearts Together Again

When love is lost, divorced people often find total fault with the other person and marriage, and question their judgment, which, in turn, may color their future choices. Married people who are widowed tend to think about what might have been instead of what was, and can find themselves stuck in the past.

Each of us dedicated our hearts to our husbands. Being in love brought a sense of yearning and security. When that was gone for each of us, our hearts and heads had to deal with enormous pain and a new reality.

Every loss is special, and each of us experienced different horrific storylines, finding ways to grieve, cope, reemerge, and fantasize how we'd find happiness—and maybe even love again.

Having gone through a loss has taught us valuable lessons. It has made us much more sympathetic to anyone alone, whether from a similar loss or out of choice to remain unpartnered. Although we both liked to think we included single friends to do dinner or a movie on Friday and Saturday nights, we now make more of a conscious effort to do so rather than make lunch plans with women without a partner— something that we often experienced. We try not to offer vague, ambiguous invitations to single friends—"I'll call you," or "Let's get together"—unless we really mean it.

Since she became single, friends began telling Barbara what a risk taker she had become. She never felt so, since for her bravery meant swishing down slopes like freestyle Olympic ski champions, hang gliding, or eating something strange looking and unknown. But they marvel that she got on planes to meet new romantic possibilities in distant cities and kept up her optimistic outlook. Her retort always was, "It's just one date."

She also knew all would be great writing material. She went overboard with her writing, pushing herself to find new opportunities she had long wanted to pursue but never had found the time. Now, she had too much time—big blocks in the evening and on weekends. She also wanted as much work as possible to help her financially. She went back to painting, which she had pursued in college and graduate school; played the piano more often; went for lots of therapy to keep moving forward and stop replaying lost possibilities; took swing dancing classes and learned to garden. Bridge was next on her list. Her biggest risk was moving to a new community, far from her roots where she knew almost nobody.

Barbara was able to relinquish her hurt toward her former husband, both for herself and their daughters' sake. She reached out on her own when their younger daughter became engaged to offer a mazel tov and encouraged him to work with her on the wedding weekend. With their daughters' urging, they had lunch as a foursome before the start of the wedding events, walked the bride down the aisle together, with Barbara first joking, "Can you believe we're doing this together?" Yet, her heart still ached when each stood alone to offer toasts, unlike the groom's long-married parents.

Fortunately, they reached a cordial level that included e-mailing each other on various milestone occasions or when something or somebody in common surfaced to recall their connection. They discussed their daughters at times when important such as their careers and dating choices or came together for certain events, sat next to one another (with Barbara's "beau" on her other side) at a dinner to toast one daughter's post-PhD hooding ceremony, and waited together, along with their son-in-law's family, in what seemed an eternity for their first grandchild to be born. Friendship would be a far stretch, but 31 years is some kind of glue that even a rancorous divorce can't—and shouldn't—remove. She also came to understand the wisdom of doing so after she read

Diane Kelly's blog titled, "Here's What Breaking Up Does to Your Brain." Kelly wrote that breaking up can make you go a little nuts due to conflicting neural systems and alluded to neuroscientist Lucy Brown, who suggests trying a little memory rewriting. "When the thought of that person comes up, instead of thinking how great [the relationship] was, think about how bad that person was for you instead'" (Kelly 2015).

Maybe, that's what you should do scientifically, but Barbara found it better and healthier to focus on the good, know that some things just don't have the staying power of a forever, and to find a relationship that would, so everyone could win.

What helped shake Margaret back into reality were her three children, a mother, and a mother-in-law who depended on her. Also, returning to her full-time job and old routine was a blessing. She didn't realize it at the time, but when her boss begged her to return, she was throwing a lifeline to rejoin the living. Once again around people, she felt more energized and less alone. With more time on her hands and on her own, she started doing something that she was unused to doing—focusing on herself. That meant seeing friends more often for a drink or a chat, writing more, playing and singing music, volunteering, taking classes, going to concerts, eating out, futzing in her garden, and taking long walks.

Slowly, she began to make new friends, start new activities—hobbies like Pilates—and learn more about wine. She went to a chiropractor-cum-sleep expert, began to cook and entertain, tried new restaurants, had her first facial and pedicure, had only her second massage, and went on her first trip with a man who wasn't her husband. She created a weekly schedule that worked well for her. She liked the routine. It was predictable and pleasurable.

Taking care of her now-deceased mother had become a part-time job. She was the point person by default because she and her mother lived in the same city; her three siblings and two of her three children lived out of town. Margaret saw her mother at least three times a week, and tried to have dinner with her on Sundays. She was in charge of most decisions affecting her mother's health and shared with one sister minimally in paying bills. Although Margaret had one son living in the same city, because of his demanding job, which required travel, she felt it was unfair to burden him with her mother's care, unless an emergency occurred.

When Nolan died, Margaret lost so much more than companionship. No more of his fabulous barbecued ribs, buttered popcorn, grilled lemon salmon, and fat juicy burgers accompanied by just the right wines he carefully selected from their basement cellar. She will always mourn the fact that he died too soon, which he told her as he was dying in the hospital, "I'm 68. Too young to die." And he was. There was so much more life that he wanted to live.

We know life is shorter than we once knew intellectually, that we must grab onto happiness any way we can, rather than wait for tomorrow, be grateful for what we have—and we have much. And we need to be there for others and also each other.

We—Barbara and Margaret—now have each other's backs. We still run our lives by each other weekly, sometimes daily, and even multiple times a day. We continue to laugh hysterically as we learn more about ourselves and our evolving styles, work, friendships, and relationships. We regularly speak now about navigating our lives further as we age and head toward our final resting places, but joke that first we'd like to gather a table of our favorite pals to sit together nightly at an assisted-care facility in the same city, if we're fortunate to reach old age and still be close pals. We can't imagine a different ending. However, we've both learned that endings can change.

REFERENCE

Kelly, Diane. "Here's What Breaking Up Does to Your Brain." *throb.gizmodo* (blog), July 20, 2015. http://throb.gizmodo.com/heres-what-breaking-up-does-to-your-brain-1717776450.

BIBLIOGRAPHY

Bergen, Candice. *A Fine Romance.* New York: Simon & Schuster, 2015.

Berman, Laura. *Real Sex for Real Women: Intimacy, Pleasure & Sexual Wellbeing.* London: Dorling Kindersley, 2010.

Bowman, Emma. "When the Sharing Economy Brings Unexpected Experience." NPR, April 27, 2015.

Ellin, Abby. "Matchmakers, Help Those Over 60 Handle Dating's Risks." *New York Times,* March 28, 2014.

Gilovich, T., Savitsky, K., & Medvec, V. H. "The Illusion of Transparency: Biased Assessments of Others' Ability to Read One's Emotional States." *Journal of Personality and Social Psychology* 75, no. 2 (1998): 332–46. doi: 10.1037/0022-3514.75.2.332. Retrieved July 20, 2011.

Kelly, Diane. "Here's What Breaking Up Does to Your Brain." *throb.gizmodo* (blog), July 20, 2015.http://throb.gizmodo.com/heres-what-breaking-up-does-to-your-brain-1717776450.

Radziwill, Carole. *What Remains: A Memoir of Fate, Friendship and Love.* New York: Scribner, 2007.

Ratner, Rebecca K., and Hamilton, Rebecca W. "Inhibited from Bowling Alone." *Journal of Consumer Research.* First published online: May 28, 2015. DOI: http://dx.doi.org/10.1093/jcr/ucv012 ucv012.

INDEX

ABOUT THE AUTHORS

Barbara Ballinger is a freelance writer who focuses on real estate, design, entertaining, and family business topics. She graduated from Barnard College and started her writing career at *House & Garden's* specialty magazines, then worked as a business reporter at a metropolitan newspaper, and as a senior editor at *Realtor Magazine*, the official magazine of the National Association of Realtors. She has written for such publications as the *New York Times, Chicago Tribune, House Beautiful, Travel & Leisure*, and *Edible Berkshires*. Barbara Ballinger was married for 31 years and has two daughters.

Margaret Crane, now a freelance writer focusing on business, food, wine, fashion, and home furnishings, is nationally known. She holds a bachelor of journalism degree from the University of Missouri. Her byline has appeared in a wide variety of publications, including the *New York Times, Newsweek, Realtor, St. Louis Business Journal, St. Louis Post-Dispatch Magazine, Midwest Living*, and *Wine Spectator*. This is the eighth book Margaret Crane has coauthored with Barbara Ballinger, and the two write a weekly web blog, *Life Lessons at 50 Plus* (http://www.lifelessonsat50plus.com). She was married 42 years to her late husband and has two sons and a daughter.